WOW, GOD!

God Bless You!

Cheryl Wilson

Wow, God!

Cheryl Wilson

Wow, God!

TABLE OF CONTENTS

PRELUDE

This book is about all the miracles that I experienced in my life from the time I was born until the present day. Every story is true. I lived through it, experienced it, and many times was 'wowed' by the very presence of God.

I pray this book will encourage you, as every time I read and re-read I was encouraged all over again myself to remember all that God has done for me. As I walked through family matters, financial difficulties, and illnesses and not just one, the faithfulness of God is what got me through the hardest and darkest times of my life. Overcoming fear, overcoming obstacles and situations that only God could do the impossible in my life and He did. The joy that came in the midnight hours and peace that walked me through the valley of the shadow of death witnessing the miraculous in my life over and over again. Stepping out of my comfort zone, being radical for Jesus. Plans changing, not understanding but believing and trusting God that His plans were far beyond anything I could ever imagine.

1

MOTHER'S FAITH

It was in the fall time of the year in the southern town of Savannah, Georgia. I was born on October 1, 1959 with what was called a plastic hip. The doctor told my parents that I would be crippled all my life. I would have to wear a brace on my leg and never be able to run or walk like normal children. I was around 3-4 months old when God healed me. The second most amazing thing that happened in my life; the first and most amazing thing was when I asked Jesus into my heart. The healing that took place would change my life forever; when the hand of God touched me.

My mother and father began praying for God to heal me. They were Christians and believed in God the Father, Jesus the Son, and the Holy Spirit. They believed that if you ask for anything in Jesus' name and believe; it shall be done. You can say to this mountain be moved and it shall be moved. **Matthew 21.21 KJV 'Jesus answered and said unto them, "Verily I say unto you, If ye have faith, and doubt not, ye shall not only do this (which is done) to the fig tree, but also if ye shall say unto this mountain, Be thou removed, and be thou cast into the sea; it shall be done."'** They exercised their faith and I am so thankful that they did. My mother told me that my hip would move in and out of the socket and that I never smiled; like I was in pain. When God healed me my hip did not come back out anymore. It happened one night after my mother had been crying out to God, praying until something happened. They had been at a revival and she wanted to go up and have me prayed for, but for some reason, the way the service went she did not get to have me prayed for. When she got home she was so discouraged as she really believed if she could just have me prayed for I would be healed. My dad had a headache and asked my mom to pray for him. My mother prayed for my dad and his headache instantly went away. My mother said if God can heal your headache being a grown man, he certainly would heal a baby who is crippled. Thank the Lord for the faith that my Mother had. So they prayed right there in that room for God to heal me from being crippled all my life, and you know what, God healed me that very night. She knew God had healed me but she needed something to hang on to when the devil would come against her and try to say I wasn't healed. My dad had went on to bed so he was sound asleep when God spoke audibly to my mother and said, 'God has healed your baby, GOD HAS HEALED YOUR BABY, **GOD HAS HEALED YOUR BABY'.** Three times God said this to my mother and each time a little louder until the room was like thunder. It was evidently meant for only my mother to hear as my dad slept right through it. When my mother took me back to the doctor he did not want to believe I was healed and said for her to put a brace on me to wear as it would help my legs. My mother put it on me on for 30 days and went back to the doctor. He kept working with me and shaking his head saying it must have something to do with that dream you had but my mother did not have a dream it was real; she was wide awake. I was eight months old before the doctor would take an x-ray and it proved I was healed. The doctor said I was well and he couldn't believe it. **Proverbs 3.5 KJV 'Trust in the Lord with all thine heart and lean not unto thine own understanding'.** So, she threw the brace in a chest-drawer where it stayed for many years.

We lived on North Gate Drive in downtown Savannah off Victory Drive in a little two bedroom brick home until I was 7. My daddy worked at Southern Bell Telephone Company. I am the second of five children; four girls and a boy. The fifth child came along after I got married. We were like doorsteps. My mother was a stay-at-home mom and she took really good care of us. She sewed and gardened and was the perfect homemaker for our family. My mother never worked outside of the home but she was involved in church, vacation bible school, prayer meetings, bible studies, visitations and nursing home ministries, prison ministries; always ready to serve the Lord anyway she could.

During those first few years I gave my mom and dad a fit. I was so fearful. I was afraid of everything. If a doll's head came off I was scared my head was going to come off. I had very abnormal fears. I was afraid of the dark, afraid of the moon, afraid of my shadow. I had a lot of growing pains as I grew with my legs hurting. The devil tried my parents through me but God had healed me and it was evident.

I gave my heart to Jesus when I was 5-years-old. At that time, we were going to a church called Evangel Temple. It was right in the middle of downtown Savannah; not the best area of the city. One night in particular, when we were at church I remember being taken out by my dad, as I was crying. The reason I was crying was I said, 'Daddy I am afraid to live forever' and he tried to explain to me that living forever is a wonderful thing and that I should not be afraid to live forever. I certainly did not want to die but I just could not comprehend living forever and it scared me. I know now as an adult why that was; it would not be evident for many more years to come. We were grounded in the church and the Lord and were taught if you were bad you would go to hell. So I guess in my little mind I was bad and living forever in hell was a horrible thought. If you are a child and you don't understand about right and wrong as we have to be taught, then you could understand why I was afraid of living forever. What I do know is God healed me of being crippled all my life. I am so thankful for a praying mother and daddy.

As I grew, this fear grew within me more intense. I had a good home life. My parents took us to church and taught us about

Jesus. We had family devotions every night and took turns reading and prayed together. We would end with the Lord's prayer or the 23rd Psalm. Many nights after we were put to bed, I would get back up scared and afraid, my heart would be racing from the fear I was feeling. I would get spanked almost nightly due to crying to sleep with my parents or just have a light on, keeping them up on a nightly basis. Something usually was said, or I saw something on TV, or someone got sick, and when I would lay down at night all these thoughts would haunt me. I remember hearing someone saying, not knowing really what I heard but my ears tuned in to, 'she swallowed her tongue', which is a term they use when someone has seizures. I went to bed that night holding my tongue afraid that I would swallow my tongue. My dad would explain to me there is no way you could swallow your tongue Cheryl. I would say then why did I hear that and what did it mean, I couldn't get past the thought of swallowing my tongue. My fear was real and I was more afraid of the dark than getting spanked to stay in the bed and go to sleep.

I remember kneeling down beside my dad after he would talk to me and try to explain to me I didn't need to be afraid and that I needed to calm down and go to sleep. I would repeat a prayer after him and I would then be able to go to sleep. If I heard someone got sick, I was sure I was going to get it. When I was about 12 years old I was delivered from this fear. It all came down when a little boy dropped dead at school that had been our neighbor. It was at Christmas time. I was horrified, a child died the same age as me and he just dropped dead, now I knew I was certainly going to die too. All the things bad I had done or had been done to me I decided I had to tell my mom. I had to confess. I wanted to make sure I would not go to hell if I died.

One of those things was a secret I had kept and I believe was the culprit of my fear of living forever. What I told my mom would be very hurtful to her and she would not tell my daddy until after her father passed; a secret my mom and I kept for many years. I was molested by my grandfather, her dad. Can you imagine the horror of this, someone she totally trusted her children with and now this. How was she to handle this? She took it to God and He healed her heart and made a way for her to deal with it. At this time I had been baptized in the Holy Ghost with the evidence of speaking in tongues. I would read the Bible and find scriptures about fear and was trusting God more in my life, but this fear had to go. We were having a revival in our home and I would go up every night for prayer and on the last night of the revival the fear left, gone in Jesus' Name. I was no longer tormented. I was set free. Jesus freed me from this fear. **Psalm 34.4 KJV 'I sought the Lord, and he answered me; he delivered me from all my fears'.** My grandfather was a Christian when he passed and I forgave him as well as my mom.

2

TENNESSEE BOUND

My family and I always loved the mountains and every summer we would go to a place called Black Rock Mountain State Park and stay in a cabin on top of the mountain for two weeks straight. There were no televisions in the cabins so we had two weeks of nothing but family time. I remember these vacations as being a wonderful time in my life. My oldest sister and I would play board games with mom and dad. We always had a puzzle out and just lots of other games and books and toys and things to do. We did lots of hiking and daddy loved to fish, so we fished at fresh trout farms and went swimming in cold mountain lakes. Daddy loved to drive around and just see all there was to see. Happy, happy times.

We always found a church to go to while on vacation. We went on Sundays and Wednesdays just like if we were home and so we made many friends at the Mountain City Church of God. We would bring friends home on Sundays and mom would cook just like we were at home.

We loved that area and wished to move there but there was no place for daddy to transfer with his work. Dad and mom wanted to move to the mountains and so they prayed for God to open that door if it be His will. Somehow the Lord led my parents to Athens, Tennessee. It wasn't where we originally wanted to end up, but God knew where He wanted us to be. I remember mom and dad made several trips looking for a place. They ended up buying 18 acres of land out in the middle of nowhere so it seemed to us, but we were so excited. The nearest neighbors were a half mile away. It was an adjustment at first as we were used to being close to our neighbors. We felt like we were on 'Little House on the Prairie' as we would get off the bus and walk across the field.

I really loved moving there. We built a house on the back part of the land and it was the first time I would have my own room. During the time of daddy getting transferred and the house selling we would make many trips on the weekends. Daddy would get off from work on Friday and we would drive the six hour drive. He would work on Saturday on the house and then on Sunday we would go to church. Daddy did not work on Sunday, even after driving all that way to work on the house. It was an exciting time in our life, felt like a vacation in a sense. We found a church that we fell in love with; Woodward Avenue Church of God. We finally got to move in the fall of 1975. This is where I needed to be to meet my future husband, Robert Allen Wilson.

I had struggled in school as we lived during the time of integration, so when we lived in Savannah, before we moved, I had to be bused to an integrated school so the blacks and whites could learn to live together equally. It was a scary time for a young girl like me and this is one of the reasons I wanted to get out of Savannah. I really did not like school but when I got to Tennessee it was so different from how things were in Savannah. I still wanted to get out of school as fast as I could and so it ended up I graduated that May in 1976 with enough credits. I never did have to go to the twelfth grade. That was a miracle as I didn't have the best grades and instead of maybe having to catch up from moving to another school I ending up graduating from the eleventh grade. I was 16 years old and graduating from high school after moving to a new city. I loved being in Athens,

Tennessee. I was so excited to see what God had in store for me. I knew God had a plan for my life.

3

CAR ACCIDENT MIRACLE 1976

I had graduated from high school and enjoyed the summer with friends and family that came to visit from Savannah. It was a good summer but when fall came I needed to get a job so I could buy a car; every teenager is dreaming of their first car. I wasn't planning to go to college, as I was just happy to get out of school and work to buy a car. I got a job as a cashier at Rose's Department Store. This was my first job. I got my driver's license right after I turned 17 and so I would drive my parents' car some or they would take me to work.

Daddy had a blue Chevrolet and one day I wanted to drive to Etowah to see a friend from church. On this particular day, my sister Cindy had stayed home from school and wanted to go with me, but mom said no she is home from school sick so she has to stay home. I went by myself which was a good thing. On the way back from my visit the road was under construction and being new at driving I was going too fast. I had just heard the thought, 'What if your wheel dropped off' and about that time I wrecked. I ended up totaling my parents' car and another car. I actually hit two cars. I am thankful that no one was hurt bad. If my sister had of been with me, things would not have been so good for her, as the whole passenger side was crushed in.

I remember the moment the car stopped I thought, 'am I dead'? I remember crawling out the window and looking at what just happened, my neck was hurting, but I was okay. I just had a whiplash. I rode in the ambulance to get checked out and called my mom when I got to the hospital. She came and got me with a neighbor, as I had the other car and dad was still at work out of town in Harriman. This was on a Wednesday and normally we would be going to church but since I had a wreck and we were all shaken up we stayed home.

It turns out Robert Wilson was coming over unannounced to see about dating me. My sister and his sister had been talking and relaying messages that we had said to tell each other. It was that night that the sparks began to fly between us. If we had not been home would he have come another night? I don't know, I just know what the enemy meant for bad God used for the good in my life. I was about to date my future husband. I ended up asking him to a hayride that our church was having and it was the start of our relationship.

4

VISION OF CHILDREN

Rob was a very good young man and knew about God but had never gone to church and had never asked Jesus into his heart. I invited him to church with me that first Sunday after he went with me to the hay ride with my church. He says he mainly went to be with me not really understanding what was about to take place in his life. It was that Sunday that he gave his heart to the Lord. His life was forever changed. He wanted more of Jesus. He wanted all that God had for him. One night not long after he got saved we were at my house and he asked my mom and dad about praying for him to get the Holy Ghost. We laid our hands on him and started praying for him. The Holy Spirit overcame him, and he went into what we call falling out in the Spirit. He was out about 30 minutes or maybe longer and while he was out God gave him a vision. **Acts 2.17 KJV 'And it shall come to pass in the last days, saith God, I will pour out of my spirit upon all flesh: and your sons and your daughters shall prophesy, and your young men shall see visions, and your old men shall dream dreams'.** He really couldn't describe it in detail as what he saw was so intense. He did tell us it was about children in a far away country that were hungry and poor and hadn't heard the story of Jesus. He said it was so bad what he saw. He also received the Holy Ghost that night with the evidence of speaking in tongues. I knew at that moment if I married him we would be involved in missions and travel to far away countries. I knew he was my soul mate from the time I laid eyes on him. We dated for a year and a half and were married on March 4, 1978.

5

SAWMILL MIRACLE

We were married a year when we found out we were expecting our first child. She was born in the fall of the year on October 30, 1979. We had just brought our daughter, Amanda Dawn Wilson home from the hospital. It was such a happy time in our lives. We were so excited to be new parents and starting our family. We had decided to stay at my parents' home for a week before trying it alone with our new baby. Rob's parents had recently bought a sawmill and Rob had decided to go over and try it out. This was one of those days that he didn't stick to the rules about safety evidently because he did not turn off the saw when he should have. I wasn't there but this is the story that he told me.

While he was sawing some lumber a board got stuck and he needed to remove it. Not seeing the danger of doing so with the saw still running he proceeded to lean over to take care of it. While doing this the saw starting coming towards him. There was no time for him to get out of the way before the saw came. He does not know how he did not get his legs cut off or worse that day except God was watching over him and sent His angels to protect Him. **Psalm 91.11 KJV 'For He shall give his angels charge over thee, to keep thee in all thy ways'.** He was wearing overalls and the saw came right across the front of him and only cut off his pocket on the front. He saw what could have been a very bad accident turn into a miracle of God. I praise the Lord for sparing Rob's life that day and allowing him not even to be hurt. It scared him so bad he quit and came home to see me and Amanda and be thankful for what God has given him. This would be one of the first miracles that Rob encountered in his life.

Four years later God blessed us with a beautiful bouncing baby boy, Branden Allen Wilson. Rob was so excited he now has a son. He said, the day that he was born, 'I have a son' with such love and excitement. We had the perfect family, a girl and a boy, what we talked about we wanted in our plans for our future when we first married. God had given us the desires of our heart with our little family. Rob was such a good father and enjoyed the time he could spend with us. He worked hard to make a living for us, but he always put God first, then family, then work, and church and in that order. We honored God and dedicated both our children back to him, raising them to know Jesus and taking them to church and reading the Bible with them nightly. We realized early on that our lives were all about God and not us. As we put God first in our lives he blessed us beyond measure. We did it because we loved Him and our hearts would just want to praise Him every day, talking to God and seeking Him for His direction in our lives. **Hebrews 11.6 KJV 'But without faith it is impossible to please Him; for he that cometh to God must believe that He is, and that He is a rewarder of them that diligently seek Him'.**

As we diligently sought Him I believe he rewarded us with our family. Children are a gift from God. Our reward is in Heaven but we receive rewards along the way when we have the faith to believe first of all and believe that He is and then seek His will in our lives diligently, not just sometimes but always.

6

OBEYING IS BETTER THAN SACRIFICE

It all started in the Fall of 1993, one October day while my husband Rob was on the job working. The Lord came to him while he was on his knees prepping a floor. He said to him, 'What are you doing here I have a work for you to do'. Rob came home and told me we have to be about the work of the Lord. I don't know how, but we must seek His face and be sensitive to where he wants us to go and when. We seemed to be in a routine of raising our family knowing in our hearts that missions was part of what we felt God had for us to do, but didn't really know how that would come about. Rob and I both had already been to Guatemala and Rob to Honduras several times so we felt that would be one of the places.

Now we had several bills and lived from paycheck to paycheck and had everything we needed to take care of our family and our needs, just didn't seem to ever have more. Rob was self employed and I worked at the hospital so taking off work or even quitting my job would be a sacrifice, but obeying to follow the Lord to where He wanted us to go was most important in our hearts. **1 Samuel 15.22 KJV 'And Samuel said, "Hath the Lord as great delight in burnt offerings and sacrifices, as in obeying the voice of the Lord? Behold, to obey is better than sacrifice and to hearken than the fat of rams."'** Our church has been involved in missions since 1987 when Rob went on his first trip to Honduras.

In January of 1994, we were able to go to Honduras and take Amanda and Branden on a two-week mission trip. It was a miracle that we could take off from our jobs let alone have money for the tickets for all four. The Lord provided and it was amazing how it all came together for our whole family to go right after Christmas. When I think back now the month of January has always been a hard month financially, so you must understand this was a miracle and God ordained it to even happen that we all got to go and go for two weeks. It was an amazing trip. We heard from the Lord on that trip to go to Central America that summer. We did not know how that would happen, but the Lord said to go and we came back from that trip and started making preparations to go.

Things started happening to get our finances in order where we could take off the summer. My husband had said we need to raise support, now at this time I had a problem with that and said, 'No, if the Lord wants us to go then he will do it without us raising support'. I was stubborn because I still was not sure we would go when it got right down to it. We started getting fought by the devil so it looked like it would not work out as we cannot see in the spirit world and when you step out in faith to follow Jesus you will have opposition. One of the oppositions was I had my first mammogram that spring and lo and behold I had to go have a biopsy. It turned out alright, but it was scary and it was thought possibly to be cancer. Praise the Lord it was not. We continued to make our plans to leave for Central America that summer. I started talking to my supervisor at work about taking a leave of absence for the summer. Rob had bought a new Ford ranger truck; first new vehicle we had ever bought off the lot. God said sell it and so he sold it and bought this used 1982 Ford Bronco and I am like yuck. We have to drive that all the way to Central America? Rob says you can't go driving something nice or you will get robbed, as it is very dangerous to be traveling anyway and you do not want to stick out like you have any kind of money at all. I accepted this after I pleaded and cried and said this isn't God's will knowing deep inside that it was. I just like to make sure, you know, God speaks to me in my heart.

It was just like God to bring everything together that summer. I was driving in town one afternoon and this man that owed us some money and quite a lot just stopped me at the red light and gave me part of what he owed and said, 'I am going to pay you all of it'. God wants me to and I want to honor God. We had told him that it was okay as he was going through a hard time. God provided for him and he paid us in full of the debt. You know, we forgave him his debt then God made a way to bless him and us. We had gotten rid of all our debt except our house. We were allowed to keep our home for the moment. I was glad as this was like a test trial to see what it was God wanted us to do and be a part of. It turned out my parents and my brother John were coming, too, so it was going to be like a caravan traveling to a foreign land. They drove their truck loaded down with everything that was felt needed for the trip and we in our bronco. I think back now and I can't believe how much we packed in that bronco and still had room for all four of us. We rented our home out to three college students. I heard from a few people and these would be the ones that would make me question this myself if I let them, you know, the naysayers, 'Are you crazy renting your home to college boys'. I would say back to them as a matter of fact, 'God told me to, and that is all I know. He will take care of it, it is just material things it can all be replaced.' I can honestly say I had released it and was excited to leave it in their hands while we were gone that summer. After all I was really leaving it in God's hands. My life is in His hands. Isn't it awesome how when you are called the Lord will equip the called. We just have to have the willing heart and faith to believe that He will move mountains in our lives. God took care of every detail. **Hebrews 13.21 NLT 'May He equip you with all you need for doing His will. May He produce in you, through the power of**

Jesus Christ, every good thing that is pleasing to Him. All glory to Him forever and ever!' Isaiah 6.8 ESV 'And I heard the voice of the Lord saying, "Whom shall I send, and who will go for us?" Then I said, "Here am I! Send me."'

7

THE SUMMER OF 1994

As the time approached for us to leave, which was right after school closed for the summer we still had not raised any support. We had paid off all of our debt and had kept one credit card but did not feel like we were to go on the credit card. **Ephesians 2.10 NIV 'For we are God's handiwork, created in Christ Jesus to do good works, which God prepared in advance for us to do'.** We were going if we went without any money. We knew God would provide. We had shared at our church and they all knew we were going. By the time it was the day of departure the funds had come in from different people and we graciously accepted the help and thanked everyone. So now here we are loaded up ready to go. We were really going to do this and we did. We had borrowed a CB so we could communicate with mom and dad as we were traveling in separate vehicles following each other. This was before we ever got a cell phone or knew that we could even get one. How fast the times have changed now.

It took us six days to get to Guatemala, leaving Texas traveling all the way through Mexico, which was not a safe thing to do. We bathed the trip in prayer and trusted the Lord that He would direct our paths and take care of us even though sometimes we did not use the best judgment in our travels through Mexico. We traveled mostly in the day, as we were told to not be out after dark.

One night though after we had traveled a couple of days into Mexico we got caught out after dark. We didn't really like the places we saw to stay at and so we kept going on not really feeling afraid to be out after dark, as things seemed to feel safe in our minds. Now up to this time, after we had crossed the border, we would have checkpoints every so often where we would have to show our passport and prove we were allowed to be in the country of Mexico. The men would be dressed in uniforms, and so you could tell they were the police. On this one occasion, we were out in the middle of nowhere and there was another checkpoint, but this time the men were wearing just ordinary clothes. It was dark out now and so we felt like it would not be safe to stop. Dad and mom were in front and we got on the CB and were communicating that we should not stop but keep going as this seems to not be safe. So we kept going and the next town was about five more miles. When we got to the end of the road and stopped, the men had chased us and pulled up behind us. One man was holding a gun at Rob and said to get out of the car. At this point, I did not know if they would shoot us or if they were robbers or policemen. Rob dropped his wallet in the car and went to the back of the car. My dad could speak Spanish so he explained that we thought that they could be robbers because they were not in uniforms like everyone else that had stopped us before so we kept going. As it turned out they were really the police checking passports. When they had chased us their car got hot, so Rob had some antifreeze and gave it to them. They wanted us to go back to the checkpoint to release us to go, so we had to drive back five miles to satisfy them. I still was not sure about this feeling they are just telling us they are the police and could shoot us and that would be the end of us on this side of Heaven. Thank the Lord, they were legit and God kept us safe from being harmed or even killed that night. We learned our lesson and made sure to not be on the road after dark anymore. We arrived safely in Guatemala about six days after we left our home in Tennessee.

Guatemala 1994

While we were in Guatemala at Casa Shalom, a mission team from Woodward Church of God came to help while we were there with the Children's Homes that needed to be finished. It was so nice to see them and even Rob's mom, Charlotte was able to come on that trip. It was so good to see everyone and that Rob's mom would even get to come to Guatemala was a miracle in itself. What I enjoyed most I think is every evening we would have devotions and share about the day and have prayer together. It seemed everyone would become closer and we all needed that encouragement. This was our church family from the United States and God opened the door for them to come while we were there.

God does give us nuggets along the way when we minister to others we also get ministered to. Sometimes we don't realize it at the moment but then we look back and see how God just knows what we need and when we need it. One night we had foot washing during our devotion time with the team. When I was growing up I experienced this more, but it seems for whatever reason people are embarrassed or don't think it pertains to them. I don't know but the scripture plainly says in **John 13.12-17 KJV 'So after He had washed their feet, and taken His garments, and was set down again, He said unto them, "Know ye what I have done to you? Ye call Me Master and Lord, and ye say well; for so I am. If I then, your Lord and Master, have washed your feet, ye also ought to wash one another's feet. For I have given you an example, that ye should do as I have done to you. Verily, verily I say unto you, The servant is not greater than his master; neither he that is sent greater than he who sent him. If ye know these things, happy are ye if ye do them."'** I want to be blessed, don't you? It doesn't say you have to do this to go to Heaven, but it says you are blessed.

Earlier in the evening, while preparing supper my mom and I had disagreed about making cornbread. It kinda' hurt my feelings as I cook it one way and she cooks it another, and I must say I was proud of the way I made it. I know most of the time daughters will do things the way our mom taught us growing up, but I always liked sweeter cornbread so I made it with some sugar. On this particular night when we had the foot washing what does my mom do but come to me to wash my feet. At first I am like to myself 'no don't come wash my feet' I wanted to still sulk in my hurt feelings but God doesn't want us to hold any hard or hurt feelings. It was a beautiful moment, my mom washing my feet and the forgiveness I felt towards her. What if we had not had the foot washing that night, would we have resolved this or carried it further into the next day. I want to believe we would have made up but not the way that this humbling experience brought us together. I was always taught by my parents, don't let the sun go down on your wrath. **Ephesians 4.26 & 27 KJV 'Be ye angry and sin not; let not the sun go down on your wrath. neither give place to the devil'.** I would have said I am sorry before I went to bed I want to believe, but I would not have experienced this wonderful love that I have for my Savior and mom and to show that love by washing her feet and her showing me the love back by washing my feet. We miss our blessings when we don't honor God by obeying His word.

Honduras 1994

We spent four weeks in Guatemala and then drove on over to Honduras. We stayed in Honduras for four weeks. We enjoyed some time with Dr. Cruz and Elsie Cruz and their family. We spent some time at their home and met another doctor and his wife whom Rob and I stayed with them while in the city of Honduras, which was mostly on the weekends. We spent most of our time in the mountains of El Pareso, Honduras. There was a clinic there that Rob had been a part of building several years earlier. We stayed there and started another building for future teams to have somewhere to stay in this village to minister to the needs of the people, setting up clinics and going to other villages.

It was great to just be with my family and know we were right where God wanted us. I learned to eat avocados during this time. My mom and I would sit under the avocado tree and do some cross stitching while we waited for my dad and Rob to need us to mix mortar or to just help them in any way we could to get the job done. We would also cook the meals and wash the clothes by hand and that was when we had to stay for two weeks in the mountain and would run out of clean clothes otherwise. It is a wonder the avocados didn't fall on our heads as they were falling all around us as we sat right under the tree. We had taken groceries with us but we were there for two weeks at a time and the stores were about two hours away in San Pedro Sula. We could get milk and eggs and tortillas but otherwise we were very limited in what we could get. Towards the end of those two weeks we were getting low on snacks and things that were easy to fix and so I started eating the avocados. You just mix them with some lemon and salt and put it on a tortilla and wow that was a good pick me up snack and so good for you.

Amanda and Branden really enjoyed playing with the kids in the village. We trusted them to not run off. One evening as it was starting to get late and I hadn't really noticed that I hadn't seen Amanda. Branden came up to me and said, 'Mom I am getting worried, Amanda went horse-back riding into the mountains and she is not back yet'. I may have known she was horse-back riding but they decided to go further and Branden and John chose not to go. We then investigated further on whom she went with and they assured us she would be safe, but Rob and I were very concerned and started praying for her safety. I thank God that he brought her back safe and before dark. It is a scary feeling to know your 15 year old daughter has ridden off on a horse with another Spanish speaking teenager girl and not know who and what might try to harm them. We were so glad to see her, but she was in trouble and didn't really understand the danger she put herself in.

After we had been in Honduras for a month we made our way back to Guatemala to start our way back home. On our way back home, unbeknownst to us since we did not have access to television, and if we did not many English channels, we did not know that a hurricane was headed right through Mexico in the area that we would be driving through. When we got to this little town called Veracruz our bronco just quit, would not move, so we had to spend all day there while the mechanics worked on our vehicle. Finally, after late in the afternoon we were able to leave and wanted to get on down the road a ways before spending the night. Not far down the road a hurricane had sweep through unknown to us. There was a great big transfer truck turned over, with like an ocean of water on each side of the road. Had we continued as we had planned we would have been right smack dab in the middle of that hurricane. I believe God protected us from that storm by detaining us in that city just several miles up the road to save us from possible harm.

We spent the night in Veracruz Mexico. The next morning we were on our way to Texas and the United States. We traveled a few more days before we got to Texas. While in Texas, another miracle happened. We had eaten breakfast and were heading on down the highway. I was driving when I started smelling something was burning like rubber or exhaust. At the same time, Rob said to me to pull off the road and he would check the vehicle. He got out and checked and couldn't see anything. When he got back into the vehicle, it would not go so we had to call a wrecker. We got into the wrecker with the man who was driving the wrecker. Amanda and Branden got in the truck with dad, mom and John. It wasn't even two minutes after we were on the road with our vehicle being towed that one of the tires rolled off the car and was going all over the interstate. It was a miracle a bad wreck didn't happen then or had we not have stopped the vehicle when we did we would have been in the bronco when the wheel came off and could have been in a very bad wreck. God kept us safe that day and others who could have been involved and kept the tire from causing a wreck. We are so thankful for the miracle that occurred in our life that day. God kept us safe.

During our whole trip, many times we were in harm's way but God intervened each time. What an amazing trip that was to see

God work the miracles in our lives. I know without a shadow of a doubt they were miracles. I lived them. I experienced them. I felt the presence of God when He intervened on our behalf. What a summer it was! To spend time with the children at Casa Shalom and the people in Honduras, to love on them and let them know that they have a future and a hope in Jesus. To have been able to spend that time with my children, who were then 11 and 15, and for them to experience God in a way that was forever implanted in their minds. I want to remember all His goodness and strength He gave us and still gives us. He even sent my parents with me and that was another moment in time I will always be grateful to my Lord and Savior for experiencing an amazing summer with my parents and my family.

8

ANOTHER MIRACLE

On another mission trip after the summer of 1994, a few years later, we got another Team together and took another mission trip to Guatemala. We experienced this miracle. One afternoon my brother John and Tommy with the Team were moving some stuff from one house to another at Casa Shalom. John was driving the truck while Tommy was in the back. It was quite steep going up the hill and somehow Tommy fell off and hurt is leg really bad. It looked to be broken and he was in a lot of pain, shouting, 'It is broke, I know it is broke'. He was carried up to the main house, since that was the closest building to get him to, and where some of the Team were staying. Everyone stopped what they were doing and gathered around and we prayed. While we prayed his leg instantly healed right in front of us. I saw it happen with my very own eyes. He just got up and walked like nothing ever happened to him. No pain, healed in Jesus name. We all rejoiced at what we experienced that afternoon. God healed Tommy and we experienced the healing power of God that day in a mighty way.

9

THE DAY HE WORE MY CROWN

We were very active in our church and we both sang in the choir and Rob was also on the Church and Pastor's Council for many years as well. He also taught Junior Church and I was involved with Bluebells and helped some as well in Junior Church. We participated in the Life Care Center taking church to the elderly and ministering every Sunday for many years during our Sunday school time. Rob would preach and I would play the piano and sing. Rob also participated in the Jail Ministry. We also headed up Crossroads Ministries for three years; ministering to the people with Hurts, Hangups, and Habits, implementing the 12 step program thru Celebrate Recovery. I know now it was a time of preparing where God was taking us, definitely out of our comfort zone.

We loved to be a part of the Christmas and Easter musicals every year. It was like we were all one big family and those memories are so beautiful to have. I will always cherish bringing our children up in that environment of the unity a church family can experience if they will just make themselves available to minister in their local church. There is plenty to be done in the body of Christ. We are all called to go out and share the love of God with one another.

One Easter, it was decided that we would put on the drama, 'The Day He Wore My Crown'. It was a pretty intense play and took lots of planning and work to get it all together. After all, this is the story of Jesus and how He died on the cross to save us from our sins. What He went through for us because He first loved us and would have died if even just for one. Rob was asked if he would play the part of Jesus. It was such an honor to him to play Jesus. He took it very serious. This would be the start of at least 12 years that he played Jesus in this drama. It was a time of coming together and praying for souls and seeing souls saved. Many people in the community would come out every year. The church would be packed. It would hold 700 or more people and it would be packed every night on a 3 day sometimes 5 day schedule. It was the year that we had moved into our new gym and that more props were made and many additions to make the play come to life even more.

This year Rob would be lifted up to the ceiling in the ascension scene to make it even more affective. I was a little apprehensive about lifting him up at the end. I was assured it would be safe. Everyone was talking about it and every night was full. It was on the last night of the play that year and the final scene, the ascension scene, that the equipment malfunctioned or something went wrong and all of a sudden it broke and he came crashing down from the very top of the gym way up high. The lights quickly went out at the same time as this was the end of the play. It was a scary feeling to know he fell and not sure how he landed or if he landed on one of the children that were right under him. It was a miracle that he didn't. You see the little children were on the stage at this time and were right under him but he did not fall on anyone.

As soon as it happened we all started praying for God to touch and heal. At first Rob said he couldn't feel his feet that they were numb, but then the feeling came back and nothing was broke. He walked out of there that night completely fine, and no one was hurt in any way. The church wanted Rob to get checked out anyway, so we made an appointment with the doctor and he confirmed he was fine. Nothing broke. The doctor said he might have a pin hair fracture and it would probably bother him when it rains. Nope, never did. He was healed and never ever had anything come from that or pain at all. Every year after that there would be church members praying for the play while it went on. It was comforting to know we were covered in prayer during the time the play was going on. I was a little nervous the next year about this scene. The ascension scene would not be taken out but they did it with rock climbing equipment from then on. He would be pulled up by some guys in the church who rocked climbed and not machinery assuring me that this was safe and they would take good care of him.

This was an awesome time in our lives, every Easter we looked forward to putting on this play. It brought us all together as a family and we loved ministering to our community. I will be forever great-ful for the heritage that this play impacted on the community and all of our family and friends who supported us and came out to participate year after year. When we did stop putting on the play it felt sad. I don't think we realized how once we stopped that we would never put the play on again. People used to call Rob, Jesus. It wasn't being sacrilegious, it was that he portrayed Jesus so well, that Rob had such a beautiful heart and spirit and really got even closer to God. In fact, after it had been a couple of years since we had put the play on someone from another church called and asked about Jesus. They said, we need Jesus. They wanted to borrow our Jesus. It was kinda funny how they called and asked about how to find Rob. The reply back to them was, we all need Jesus. He graciously accepted the invitation to play Jesus in their play. It was a smaller church so not as many could get in the church and they put it on several times, even 2-3 times on the weekend and it was full each time.

This is one of the special memories I have of my sweet husband. He loved Jesus so much. It was about seeing souls saved and not anything about himself, but about serving the Lord and doing all he could for others, reaching out.

10

TRACTOR ACCIDENT

We were planning our 25th wedding anniversary and Rob was building a house up on a mountain and if he were to fall off the roof he literally would fall off the mountain. It seems I always worry about Rob getting hurt as he is always driving tractors and climbing high to build homes. This time I was really concerned to the point that I had even asked my mom to pray for safety as I just felt we needed extra prayer for Rob during this time. It wasn't until two years later that I would find out about the accident. He knew I would have been upset but I told him he needed to tell what God had done for him and yes maybe I would have been upset but so thankful to know God spared his life again.

One morning when Rob was taking the tractor up to the house on the mountain, which was very steep, he got stuck and so he got on the tractor to back the tractor off the trailer, and when he was doing so the tractor lifted up and came back down with one tire not on the trailer. When this happened the tractor literally rolled with him on the tractor, it rolled all the way over. Rob said there was no where for him to go and that an angel had to have covered him. The smoke stack was all bent but not a scratch was on Rob. After the tractor rolled over he jumped up without a scratch not really sure what had just happened. He ran after the tractor and it had backed itself back into a bank and stalled. He then praised the Lord as he realized he should have just been killed or hurt badly, as there was nowhere for him to have been and not got crushed, but God spared his life that day.

11

FALLING OFF ROOF ACCIDENT

We always loved our vacations and always looked forward to getting some time away. Rob worked really hard and was always glad that I made sure we took vacations every year. We especially seemed more excited this time to go and spend some much-needed time together doing all the things we loved. We have a timeshare in Gatlinburg, Tennessee and we love to go, it isn't far to travel and the mountains are just so beautiful. We can never get enough of God's beauty.

It was on a Thursday just before we were to go on vacation. It was in the afternoon and just about quitting time when all of a sudden everything came crashing down and he and two other guys fell. He literally turned all the way upside down and somehow landed on his hands on concrete. Thankfully no one else was hurt, it could have been really bad. Rob broke both wrists. He said he was in so much pain that he thought he was going to pass out while the guy he was working for drove him to the hospital. The man called me and said your husband is okay but there has been an accident and I am driving him to the hospital for me to meet him there. I was a little shaky when he told me, afraid that it was really worse than what he was letting me know. I found out later how blessed Rob was to be alive or could have been paralyzed. He fell so fast that he didn't have time to think how to land just that he was able to land on his hands after he was turned upside down backwards.

When I think of what could have been, I just give God all the glory and honor and praise. He had both hands up past his elbows in casts for six weeks. We decided to go on vacation anyway since we already had the condo booked. We were in the MIP program at the time and had lots of studying we could do. Needless to say, it was a different kind of vacation than what we had planned, but it turned out to be a good vacation after all. It gave Rob time to heal some and by the next week after vacation, he didn't miss a beat. He had three jobs going and was able to drive himself with two broken wrists. He was a man that he wouldn't let anything get him down and always looked to God. He would always say to me, 'Just trust God, it is all going to be all right Cheryl' and it was. What the enemy meant for harm God turned into good. God is our healer and protector and encourager. He used this to make us stronger and to show us His glory in all of this.

12

LET GO AND LET GOD!

I really wasn't on board to purchase more land, but Rob and daddy won out this time. My dad had told Rob about this property a few years earlier when it was auctioned off thinking he might like to own it then and was really a good price. We agreed at that time not to purchase it then, bad mistake. Several years later it came up for sale again except this time the price had doubled. Daddy told Rob about it and there was no talking him out of it again. At this time, we had partnered with Rob's parents and one of his sister's and her husband to take on the farm and buying more land was to help feed the cows; a good investment so it seemed. It wasn't long before things went badly wrong and the farm had to be sold. We had also bought up other acreage that connected to the farmland and with the cows being sold we could no longer make the payment. It was not a good situation to be in. God showed favor and provided a lease-to-own buyer, it would be several years before he would buy us out and at times he would be late on the payment, which would hit our credit as we could not pay it on time. We let go and let God and He supplied our every need. I had felt very uneasy about buying the property next to mom and dad and couldn't really understand why we needed this extra expense. To me the cows had plenty of hay, did we really need more land? Our credit was so good that the banks would not tell us no, so it must be God's will, right?

Our son, Branden decided he would buy all of the 29 acres from us and built a nice home on the property. The home ended up being larger than what had initially been planned making the payment more than he could pay at this time in his life, so we agreed to take it back since we were the guarantees on the loan. We still owned our home in Englewood and could not afford to keep up two homes. It was a very stressful time. We put the home and the 29 acres on the market and had almost sold it and would have had we not heard God speak to us together one evening to build a subdivision. We heard it loud and clear. I know that sounds crazy huh! There were some people interested that very day to buy the home and we decided to take a leap of faith and not sell it. This was what we knew that God had dropped this in both of our hearts to do. It was such a liberating feeling to have the direction to move forward.

We didn't know how it was going to happen but we knew it would happen. We needed to borrow the money to put the road, electricity and water and survey and soil maps and everything that is needed to make a subdivision. The first thing is to get the approval letter that the road would be put in within a year to be able even to get the approval for a subdivision. Due to going through the farm being sold and our credit score being hit tremendously, this was even more crazy that we would not just sell and count our loses and move on. Rob being a builder and having good credit could always get loans from time to time to buy equipment, build homes, cattle, machinery, trailers, tractors, but all of this changed when the farm had to be sold. It not only hurt us financially but the family was really upset with us. It was one of the hardest times in our lives to ever go through. What we meant for good turned out to hurt us, and all of those involved. We took a pretty big hit but God was always faithful.

We did a lot of praying and crying out to God to heal our family and to heal our finances and to show us the way out. We needed a way out. It looked like everything was going to fall out from under us. We prayed God if you take it all we will still serve you anyway. We accepted whatever happens, God has a plan. Our earnest prayer was for God to heal our family and put us all back together. We were broken and hurting. We were shunned from the family for a couple of years, that was how bad it was. We would push forward and try but it was not happening so we loved them from afar during this time and prayed and cried and prayed some more. We could not believe this was happening. My husband, Rob was such a beautiful man and loved God with all his heart and loved his family and would not harm a soul. He would give you the shirt off of his back if he thought you needed it. It was during this time that we had started Celebrate Recovery every week on Tuesday nights. A program for anyone with hurts, hangups, and habits. We thought we were doing this to help others but it ended up being the best place for us to be every week to heal our hearts from what we were going thru.

One of the requirements to be able to get a subdivision approved is getting the financial part approved. If we couldn't get that then we would have been stopped dead in our tracks. We had a relationship with the banks. At this time before the economy fell, it was falling but hadn't affected us the way it did later. Our credit score was not good at all, so the only way to get this approval would be the relationship knowing us for who we were and not for what had happened with the farm. At first the banker told us he didn't think it was going to be possible to give the approval letter. We left the bank feeling low and that if it wasn't God's will then we didn't want to move forward anyway. We would figure out what we could do if this wasn't the option. We cried out to God and said we know we heard your voice on this subdivision and if it was going to happen then He had to move on our behalf. When God is in it he opens doors that are impossible. We got the call from the banker later that day and he said, at first he wasn't going to approve it but then he felt like God was speaking to him to do it. Not to look at our circumstances but to look beyond that which had happened with the farm.

When I look back now to think that we would even ask for funding after everything was a leap of faith on our part. We were praising the Lord, it was an awesome feeling to see this miracle come to pass. What you don't know that I must tell you is, we could not buy a washer and dryer on credit but could get a loan for a subdivision, a very large loan, explain that to me. There is no explanation except God and only God. This is the kind of God we serve. We praised the Lord for the impossible happening in our lives. We were walking in the favor of the Lord. Our hearts were breaking in the mist with the family situation, but God was holding us in the palm of His hand. I've got this, children, trust me, follow me, and we continued to Let go and Let God. We gave God all the glory and honor for what he was doing and about to do in our lives. **Philippians 4.19 KJV 'And my God will supply all your needs according to His riches in Glory in Christ Jesus'.**

In the middle of God moving in our lives there was still the heaviness but hope was always there knowing some way, some how God was going to heal the family situation. We just continued to put our trust in Him and walk out our life to get out of our debt. Where God led we followed. We listened to His still small voice and watched Him open the doors to be free from our debt. It would take some time but this was how Spring Creek Cove Subdivision came to be. Not in our plans originally but in God's plan. I finally realized why we were supposed to buy this property. It took several years of really knowing the purpose of buying something that was a burden in the beginning. **Matthew 11.28-30 KJV 'Come unto me, all ye that labour and are heavy laden, and I will give you rest. Take my yoke upon you, and learn of me; for I am meek and lowly in heart: and ye shall find rest unto your souls. For my yoke is easy, and my burden is light.'** When you rest in the Lord and trust Him the burden becomes easy to bear. There is good rest in the Lord.

In the mist of trials you have to rest at Jesus' feet. He is the only way you can make it. We must give it to Him. This burden in our life became bearable, the yoke became easy and the burden light.

As we moved forward with the subdivision, many doors began to open to sell the lots. We had 19 lots that spanned 29 acres. It became a private residential community protecting the investment of all who would buy in the community. The first lot that we sold was $40,000 cash deal. If you will remember when this 29 acres was auctioned off several years before and we did not purchase then was around $60,000 and we had bought it for double. Just one Lot sold and already $40,000. When God is in control the price is right. In 2008, we became a community. Not only did we get a loan for the subdivision but also a loan to build a speck house and after selling the Lot 19 home we moved into the speck home on Lot 17, built two custom homes and four families moved in. We became a neighborhood. This all happened in a span of 8 months.

My mom and dad really have enjoyed having a community behind them. Daddy loved to take walks in the neighborhood on the nice black top road, getting to know his new neighbors, inviting them to church and over to their home. The first neighbors have become like family to us. Mom had prayed for neighbors when she felt like she might want some people nearby. God heard her prayer and answered. Daddy went to be with Jesus since then and now mom has her neighbors. There are three little boys who live next door and they check on mom and bring her vegetables and other things from time to time. The sound of them playing outside is music to her ears. God takes care of His children and knows just what we have need of. Nothing is by accident. When we first moved to Tennessee it was a beautiful field next to a ridge with a creek with acres of fields and grass and cattle grazing, even a small family cemetery in a distance. We loved to go over there and run and play, a place of serenity and peace. What fond memories. It makes me smile to be a part of something good.

As the next few years went by the healing came in the family. It came kinda all at once. We never gave up trying to make amends and then one day God just healed it and we were welcomed back into the family. Another miracle that we lived thru. Hang on to what you know to be true. Stand on the promises of God. He will not fail you. **Psalms 34.4 KJV 'I sought the Lord and He heard me, and delivered me from all my fears'.**

13

GOD HAS EVERYTHING UNDER CONTROL

In the winter of 2011, I went to work part-time at Wood's Memorial Hospital in the Medical Records Department. I was at work when I felt like God was telling me to get shots, the Hepatitis B shot. I had never taken it and it was offered to me free since I worked for the hospital. That very same day, Rob had also heard from God about getting our passports renewed as they had expired. He wasn't sure how he would tell me this. So when I told him that I felt like we should get shots he then proceeded to tell me that he felt like God was telling him to get Passports. We both agreed that God was telling us we would be ministering out of the country.

I got my first Hepatitis B shot, which was the first of three in total. Before I would get my next shot I was diagnosed with breast cancer, which did not allow me to receive any more vaccines. I had to go see my GYN doctor for an infection and so he decided I needed to go ahead and get my mammogram. It was a good thing since it didn't turn out so good. I really wasn't concerned that it would be anything since I had a scare when I was 35. I had to have a biopsy and so on the day of my results I went by myself telling Rob I would be fine it won't be anything. He wasn't worried either.

I remember when the doctor told me I was like in shock. I felt like this was somebody else and not me. I even left there and went and showed a house since I was selling real estate and had already set that up for after my appointment. I had called Rob and told him over the phone and when I got to my mom's after showing a house I causally said to her, 'did Rob tell you my news', she said what news and I proceeded to tell her I was just told I had breast cancer. She prayed against it and I felt like everything would be okay.

Before, I had left the doctors office I had gone ahead and scheduled a mastectomy thinking I covered everything and did what I'm supposed to do. Isn't that what all women do, have a mastectomy when they get breast cancer? As I proceeded to tell others, different ones would say, 'aren't you going to get a second opinion?' I would say no and then it was like God said to me, why don't you at least go to the mammogram center in Chattanooga, Mary Ellen Locher Breast Center, so I made my appointment and went. It turned out I didn't need a mastectomy. The doctor said my prognosis was the same that I could keep my breast. I would still have to have chemotherapy and radiation no matter what I decided. He recommended to keep my breast and so the decision was made.

I had a lumpectomy with lymph node dissection. My diagnosis was triple negative breast cancer stage 1A, a nasty cancer but in the early stages. When I was having a test done to see if it had spread to my lymph nodes I know I heard God say to me I was healed. My family still insisted that I should take chemotherapy and radiation. The doctor explained to me it was like buckling up your seat-belt and would only give me just 15 percent more of a chance that it would not come back. I was trusting God that I heard Him tell me He healed me so I agreed.

I can't tell you how devastating this was. To hear from God about being a missionary and then get breast cancer. I started chemotherapy in the fall of 2011, which would last until December. I had initially been on a trial of Avastin, which was pulled after the first of the year. I was to have taken it for one year. When I had my surgery to remove the cancer the margins were not as clear as they wanted them so I had to have a re-excision of the area to make sure I was clean after chemotherapy and before radiation. It looked suspicious but praise God everything was clean. I had to hold off on chemotherapy to have the re-excision and when I was told no more chemotherapy I was so thankful. I just couldn't see myself going a whole year. I had lost my hair and really was looking forward to it growing back. They said that it would probably grow back while taking the Avastin but I felt sick to my stomach afraid that it wouldn't. It is a very hard thing for a woman to lose her hair. I said I would never have another bad hair day as long as I have hair. My hair came back but not as thick as it used to be. I am thankful I had thick hair and thankful my hair came back.

Right before I got diagnosed with breast cancer I had had a dream that my hair fell out in handfuls in the shower. It was so real. When I got the news and knew that it really was going to fall out for real the realization and actuality of it happening was not as scary as the dream. It came out but not so fast. I accepted it because I had to and God helped me most of all. He held my hand and was there every step of the way. While I was having chemotherapy I felt His love surround me, such a peace of knowing if I die I am going to a better place. During this time, God was preparing me for the future. He was making me stronger than I ever knew I would need to be.

It was during this time that Rob had been talking to Dr. Popejoy about going to Romania. I had told him, 'We are not going anywhere, I have cancer!' He continued to find out all he could and even talked with my doctor about going to Romania in the middle of chemotherapy. We were looking at going in the summer of 2012 to see what God was telling us about Romania. He even got my doctor to agree I could go even while on the study drug Avastin. I couldn't believe it and wasn't sure I would want to go, but God took care of it because the study drug was pulled and I was finished with all my treatment by that summer. We would not go until October due to it not being the right time to go. It is all in God's timing.

We went and heard from God about missions. Our hearts were ready but circumstances and more illness would detain us a while longer. It wouldn't stop us but just make us want to follow God's plan for our life all the more. It consumed us. The harder it seemed to get to be in the perfect will of God, the more our hearts were ready to just step into what God had for us to do. People can be so hard to understand and say things that really they shouldn't say and they mean well. If we had listened to people about going to Romania we would have never gone and experienced sharing the gospel on the other side of the world. There are only 2 percent Christians in Europe; most are orthodox and muslin. The Bible says **Mark 16.15 KJV 'And he said unto them, "Go ye into all the world, and preach the gospel to all creation"'**. We are all called to go and few are chosen. **Matthew KJV 22.14 'For many are called, but few are chosen'.**

We have to accept that we are chosen and pursue the call in our hearts to do what the Bible tells us to do. Just like salvation is for all but not everyone accepts therefore they reject being chosen by God. God chose us all and we are given a choice. He doesn't make us serve Him. He loves us and wants us to choose Him. It makes Him very sad when we turn away from Him. God put the desire in my heart to see others touched, healed, saved, and filled with the Holy Ghost. When the hand of God touched me, I have never been the same. He has healed me many times in my life and I am so thankful. God loves you as much as He loves me, He will do the same for you. All you have to do is open your heart to Him and let Him come in. He wants to live inside of you.

14

HE IS AN ON-TIME GOD

We had our home under contract for one year, with a contingency for the buyers to sell their home. After we got back from Romania we were going to sell everything and make our plans to go to Romania as full time missionaries in July 2013 as our leaving date. We would need six months to raise support. The year before Rob had sold his business and machines and even his truck. It was part of the plan. We were struggling and needed to sell our home, as the house payment was rather large. It was only God that kept us going. We had been trying to sell the shop and one afternoon a man called and asked if Rob was interested in selling his excavator. He really hadn't thought about it as he used it to put in septic tanks and was glad to have this to make money. There really wasn't a lot going on and it was just sitting there and we needed to pay bills. I told him, maybe you should listen to see what God is saying. It was after that that we decided to sell all of Rob's machines and equipment. I had put everything on Craigslist and we had a garage sale in the middle of winter and it was amazing all the people that came and bought. It was thought he would not get what his excavator was worth. Tell that to God. Rob sold it for a very good price. He had not planned on selling his truck but got an offer to sell it and had said to God, 'My truck too Lord'?

It was an emotional time to see him sell all his stuff and obey what he felt like God was telling him. A man and his truck and excavating equipment and woodworking machines and trailers and dump-truck. This would keep us going thru the hard times ahead and prepare us for selling everything to follow God, and following God was all that mattered. We were sold out to God and as he moved on our hearts to sell everything he showed us how to do it. There was an excitement knowing we were right where God wanted us even in the hardest time of our life there was a peace of knowing God was in control and we put our trust Him.

15

AN ANGEL ENCOUNTER

It was on the trip in October 2012 on our way to Romania. I was still not feeling I would sell it all to be a missionary. I needed something more. I needed a direct sign from the Lord, after all I had been through cancer and a survivor. I had more of a willing heart but this was very serious and I needed a serious answer.

It all started with running late to get to the airport. We had to wait on a friend to bring something by to take to Romania with us. We were still going to be all right with the time, but it makes you nervous and so we were rushing. My sister Cindy and her husband went with us to the airport to get our car. On the way while Rob was changing lanes we almost had a wreck, thankfully the Lord straightened out the car just in time so we were all a little shook up. We finally get to the airport and get checked in, our ticket had said one gate but when we got there it was wrong and so were told to go to another gate. We go to that gate and we get checked in and now we are ready, we are going to Romania.

It was maybe ten minutes and we were told that due to mechanical issues that this flight would be canceled and would not be going anywhere; to come to the desk or phone and make other arrangements. At this point, I am thinking, maybe we are not supposed to go after all. Rob gets in line for the phone and I am in line for the desk so whoever gets there first to figure out what we can do and/or get a voucher. In the meantime, the gate next to us was filled up with people everywhere. I had asked someone what was going on and they said that that flight was overbooked. Just at that moment Rob had been on the phone already with someone and there was a call over the intercom, Wilson party of two go to Gate 3 the plane is waiting for you. I said to this person sitting there, 'We are Wilson party of two but it can't be us our plane is canceled due to mechanical issues'. Just then Rob calls to me and says Cheryl come on we have to get on this plane at Gate 3, the one overbooked. I'm like okay and here we go.

As soon as we walk on the plane there are only two seats and they are not together. I walk in and the steward man says to me, 'Are you going to follow me back here?' He says it to me twice and I'm like yes, then he says would you like to sit with your husband and I am like yes that would be great. It was like five minutes literally after we set down and the plane was taking off. Just as the plane got up good in the air the steward man came back to us and knelt down beside us. We started telling him our morning and how we got here and how we almost had a wreck. He says to us, 'I know, I have got you covered', and gave us two delta wings and gives us a high five. He also asked if we would like something to drink, now they don't give drinks on this flight and weren't offering anyone else a drink at this time. He brought us both back a coke. This was a 30 minute flight to Atlanta to catch our connecting flight and for this whole 30 minutes we both felt such a presence of the Lord. I said to Rob Is that an Angel? With tears in his eyes we both agreed there was something special going on here.

We didn't realize the message until on the way home from Romania and the message was. Are you going to follow me? I know and I have got you covered. This steward could not know and what did he mean he had us covered. It was an angel I will always believe and a direct answer to my question to the Lord. I need something to know what your will is Lord in our lives. It wasn't necessarily about going to Romania so much as following the Lord and what was ahead. Yes, God knew what was ahead and He had us covered. He was letting us know in advance. I know all about your struggles but I have you covered, just trust me, struggles that we had no idea were about to enter into our lives. **Proverbs 3.5-6 KJV 'Trust in the Lord with all your heart, and do not lean on your own understanding. In all your ways acknowledge him, and he will make straight the paths.' Psalm 46.1 KJV 'God is our refuge and strength, an ever present help in trouble'.**

16

FALLING STAR

It had been two weeks now since we had been back from Romania and our hearts were ready to sell everything and go to Romania as missionaries. We had made the decision that we were going the next year and would start selling everything and raising our support. I was really going to start selling furniture out of the house and I was feeling a little uncertain. Why is it that we have to doubt what we know is the truth. Is it fear of the unknown? I don't get it. What I doubted was my direct message on the plane.

I was talking to Rob as we were riding home from church one night talking about the angel experience on the plane. I had decided that it was just what it was. I wanted it to be a direct message but it was just the way it turned out. It was no longer out of my mouth than we had just turned onto the next road that this huge, falling star, like it took 3-4 seconds to fall, like time froze. How can I explain it that it was just breathtaking. We both experienced it at the same time. It was like God was speaking to us both saying, 'As real as that star you just saw falling before your very eyes that the angel experience on the plane was a direct message', that it was truly an angel.

I will always believe this to be the truth. I lived it, I experienced it and it was beautiful. God is real and He is amazing and He cares for us. He wants us to trust Him with our whole life and give it to Him. Like the song says, I give myself away, I give myself away so you can use me. I give myself away. This was so in us to be used by the Lord. We wanted to give ourselves away. To die to self no matter what came our way, because this message was a comfort in all the things that were ahead. God knew and He had us covered and we stood on that in all the trails we encountered. 'We are following you Lord, no matter what happens we are following you Lord. We love you and we honor you in all that we say and do. It is not about us it is about Him.'

17

What Is This?

It all started in November 2012 around Thanksgiving right after we got back from our trip to Romania. Rob complained of his neck being swollen with a definite hard place in the lymph node. It was very painful. Our daughter, Amanda, who is a medical doctor, took a look at it while they were in for Thanksgiving. She did not like how it felt and said, 'Dad if that doesn't go away I want you to get it checked out'. Shortly thereafter he took a course of antibiotics due to some bronchitis and it appeared to go away. We had our home up for sell and actually had a contract with a contingency of the buyer to sell his home first. We had just gotten the word that the contract had fallen through and we would not be selling our home to these buyers. We had decided to start selling the furniture before closing on the house thinking that everything was going to happen with selling the house and heading to Romania to be missionaries.

When this happened, I stopped trying to sell the furniture. For two weeks after that I kept feeling like God was telling me to keep moving forward and trust HIM that the home would sell and soon. We had our home on the market for three years. Several items we were starting to sell, but still no contract. This was very hard to do. I thought we are going to have an empty house. This is crazy. What are we doing? We felt the Holy Spirit telling us that it was the right thing to do. On January 1, we got a call from a realtor who had a buyer that was interested in our home. He showed it on January 2, and on January 8 we had a verbal contract and a home inspection already done. On February 8, Rob's birthday, we closed on our home. I sold my Baby Grand piano to a church out of Cleveland, Tennessee, Community Hall Church. It was the hardest part of all to see my piano sold, but God gave me peace that this was the right thing to do. It felt good to know that it would be played every Sunday in a church. I get to play it occasionally when I visit Community Hall. Pastor Jeannie has become a good friend and mentor to me. I cherish her friendship and prayers from her and the church.

In January, Rob started swelling again in that lymph node and so he went to see Dr. Sharpe who said he did not know what it was and ordered a CT scan. The CT scan indicated he needed further testing, so Rob was referred to an ENT doctor in Cleveland, Tennessee. Dr. Byrd. He told us that he would not stop until he knew what it wasn't. During this time, we had moved in with mom and dad after we sold our house, as we were raising our support with a perspective leaving date of July 9. Dr. Byrd did a needle biopsy and on the day that Rob got the news that it was cancer he was flat on his back with a stomach virus and I come in and tell him that Dr. Byrd called and said it was cancer. Rob then got his bible out and started seeking the Lord about the cancer and God gave him **2 Chronicles 20** where it talks about king Jehoshaphat facing a vast army which he could not defeat and he was afraid. The Lord told him it was not his battle that He was going to fight it. After the battle, king Jehoshaphat goes to look over the battle field and in verse 24 all he sees is dead bodies everywhere and it says in that verse not one left alive. When Rob read that the Holy Spirit spoke to Rob and said he was going to fight this battle for him too and that not one cancer cell will be left alive and he started rejoicing. He didn't know how God would do it but he stood on that promise.

In the meantime, the biopsy came back inconclusive differentiated squamous cell carcinoma, so a PET scan was ordered to diagnose things further. Rob then went to see an oncologist and a radiation doctor to start the process of chemotherapy and radiation. The radiation doctor told us he was considered to be a stage IV that this was a secondary diagnosis. It supposedly had metastasized from somewhere that chemotherapy and radiation would still need to be done regardless what the PET scan showed. The PET scan lit up Rob's tonsils so Dr. Byrd did a tonsillectomy. In the meantime, the knot on Rob's neck appeared to be getting smaller. Dr. Byrd did not even try to take it out, which probably would have been a good idea but that was not the protocol, so they said. We were believing for the miracle and that is what we got. Rob also had an abscessed tooth, which had been going on for about four years, so we wondered could that have caused this and it not really be cancer. Dr. Byrd said no but when Rob's tonsillectomy and four point biopsy came back no cancer Dr. Byrd said, call it something, call it a miracle. I know you will call it a miracle, cancer just does not go away. He checked his neck and said, 'I don't even feel anything to biopsy'. He also said I would have bet more than my lunch that your tonsils were cancerous. Praise the Lord, we were rejoicing.

He sent us to go get some breakfast while he got in contact with the pathologist who diagnosed the cancer in the first place. He had said I should release you and did cancel chemotherapy and radiation. We were on a high and started telling our story. God had healed Rob. Dr. Byrd said I want to see you back in about six weeks to check you again. This all happened in March of 2013. We told him we were leaving for Romania in July so the first of May Rob went back to see Dr. Byrd. He said, 'You know I am looking for something?' so he did a guided needle biopsy. When the biopsy came back it still showed the same diagnosis as before and Dr. Byrd said he had to recommend treatment. We did not accept this and said no, God had healed Rob and we were just going to go on to Romania and trust the Lord. About 2-3 weeks later on a Saturday night, Rob got a bad headache and woke up on Sunday morning with his face drooping like Bell's palsy. So we made an appointment to see the doctor in Cleveland, but he had to see Dr. Byrd's partner. They did another CT scan and followed up that Friday as we were on our way to Florida for vacation to spend time with the kids.

On that Friday, Dr. Byrd said the cancer was pressing on the nerve and he had to recommend treatment. Rob was like if I have to have treatment then I want to go to Alabama near our daughter, Amanda who she set us up for a second opinion. We went on to Florida to have our vacation trusting God for the miracle we knew we already had received back in March. We know God healed Rob and just continued to put our trust in the Lord and stand on HIS promises. While in Florida, I pleaded with Rob 'Let's just go back to Tennessee and do the treatment there' that it would be the best scenario and most comfortable place. Rob started experiencing some numbness and tingling down that whole side. It seemed he was getting worse. Rob said I feel so strong that we are to go to Alabama and so we proceeded in that direction.

Amanda had set up an appointment with Dr. Davidson, who was a Christian. When we were in his office waiting to be seen, Rob and I were just crying out to the Lord. We know you called us why are we dealing with cancer again? We know you healed Rob. Lord you are our healer and we thank you for healing him so what is this? Why is this happening again? When Dr. Davidson came in after looking at Rob's chart he said you guys have been on a roller coaster. He said I don't know why you have cancer or why you are here in Alabama, but I was just reading in Job this morning and he did not understand either but he trusted God. We are not ruling out surgery. We felt such a peace after talking with Dr. Davidson that God had led us to Alabama for a reason.

18

PRAY UNTIL SOMETHING HAPPENS

While out in the lobby scheduling an appointment for another PET scan, something happened that just took us by surprise. The room was full of people, maybe 15 or more, waiting also to make appointments. All of a sudden this older black man came from across the room pushing a lady in a wheelchair. He came around to where we were. As he was coming towards us he said, 'You, you there, I have a message for you'. This is what the message was, 'The miracle has begun, consider being at this place done. What God has started man cannot stop. The Lord has a mighty work for us to do.' He then looked over at me and he said for me to release it to give it to the Lord, that everything was going to be alright.

We both just started crying right there that God cared about us so much that he sent a messenger to encourage us. He also gave us the acronym PUSH, Pray Until Something Happens. It felt like we were on 'Touched by An Angel' or something. It was so real, so amazing, like a light was shining in the room that time had stopped for a moment. I had asked him who are you and he said I am a prophet. He also told me that I needed to give him a drink of water, he gave me the scripture, **Matthew 10.42 KJV 'And whosoever shall give to drink unto one of these little ones a cup of cold water only in the name of a disciple,**

verily I say unto you, he shall in no wise lose his reward', which I did. So here we are on a high again. We went back to Athens, TN until the next week when Rob would have another PET scan and see Dr. Davidson to decide if surgery was an option or not. The news was not what we wanted to hear. The cancer was too intensive and surgery would not be an option. He only recommended chemotherapy and radiation. We were like no we want surgery but went along with what Dr. Davidson recommended and proceeded to set up for a Port to start radiation and chemotherapy. We went back to Athens feeling really low and then the Lord woke Rob up at 3.00 am the next morning and said to him PUSH, (Pray Until Something Happens). We called some people and I put on Face Book anyone who wanted to come and pray at the church on that Friday night for Rob. We had around 15 people. It was good and the word we got was RECEIVE. The platter is full and all we have to do is take from it what we have need of from the Lord. We left feeling like God is about to show up again on our behalf. We went back to Alabama the next week continuing down this path of treatment but expecting a miracle.

So here we are at the radiation doctor to set that up. We are crying out to God again and asking one more time to call this off again please Lord, don't let this be. God always works on our behalf, apparently the doctor we were supposed to have seen was on vacation but Dr. Davidson said to go ahead and see whoever was available, that he needed to get started with treatment as soon as possible. Dr. Ingram said to Rob, 'You haven't seen a cancer surgeon specialist have you?' and we said 'No'. He said tell me this, you had a tonsillectomy but you had a tumor on the side of your neck that was cancerous, but they take out your tonsils? He said it twice like he could not believe it. You see Dr. Ingram is a perfectionist. He asked us if we would go see a surgeon if he could set it up and we said yes that we wanted to have it taken out if that would be the best prognosis. We were still believing that it would not be cancer if he could just have it removed. He went and made a call and then came back in and said you need to thank Dr. Withrow, he can see you tomorrow at 12.00, which it takes two months to get in to see him. We had no doubt that Rob would be having surgery. Dr. Withrow said that it needed to come out, that he wasn't 100 percent sure what it was. He did say that there was a 10 percent chance that he could lose his nerve in his face. We agreed that it was worth the chance.

On July 8th, Rob had a seven hour surgery. Dr. Withrow tried to save his nerve, but the cancer was wrapped around his nerve and when he did a frozen section revealing cancer he said he had no choice but to take the nerve. He also had cancer in the lymph nodes. He took out 40 and 27 of them were diseased. He said if the cancer had been any further down he would have had to call in a pulmonologist. For whatever reason it turned out to be cancer, but it was a totally different cancer than originally thought. This type is not known to respond to chemotherapy or radiation, but the doctors recommended hitting the areas that the cancer was removed from with radiation and chemotherapy anyway for a better prognosis. We trusted in the Lord and felt like He was taking us down this path. Dr. Ingram said if Rob had chemotherapy and radiation in March when everything appeared to have gone away probably Rob would have died. We believe in divine healing and it appears that God was using the doctors with medicine for the healing. It was a hard three weeks after surgery with Rob waking up without his nerve and the diagnosis being cancer. I remember that day we had such faith that it would not be cancer and when the chaplain came to talk to us before surgery Rob encouraged her, talking about going to Romania and very upbeat that God was working out His plan and we were just trusting in Him. He didn't want to do treatment but decided he would, since everyone was recommending it.

After Rob's second week of treatment he was getting really sick and losing weight. He said, 'I am not taking anymore treatment'. The Lord woke Rob up in the middle of the night one night before the next treatment and told him, 'This is not about you, it is about what I have for you to do, and what I did at Calvary'. So Rob felt like the Lord wanted him in the treatment room to encourage others and witness for him, so he had a different outlook from then on. He did get sicker and lost about 25 pounds, but praise the Lord he has a testimony to share with others. God is with them and that it isn't His will for anyone to be sick. We shared the love of God with others while going through our own sicknesses.

19

AMANDA HEALED

It was during the time that Rob had first got diagnosed with cancer, and everything seemed to have gone away. While we were celebrating Rob's healing that Amanda, our daughter, had gotten the news that she had blood work that showed suspicious for cancer cells in her ovaries. She needed to have exploratory surgery to confirm if it was or not. She had been in a lot of pain for about three weeks, so we were concerned and praying for her to not have cancer. It seemed that 'C' word had been going around our family much too long and we needed to break this in Jesus' name. We started bathing her in prayer and asking others to pray. She underwent an oophorectomy on that side. When they got in there it turned out to be a tubal pregnancy that had twisted and caused the ovary to die. In all reality, she could have bled to death in the three weeks it took to set up surgery. The doctor that did the surgery was baffled, he knew that it looked cancerous and when the pathology report came back a tubal pregnancy he was just amazed at the final diagnosis. We know that our heavenly father intervened on her behalf and healed her without a shadow of doubt.

20

AUTUMN HEALED

We also had a bout with Autumn, my granddaughter, with her platelets in and around all of what was going on with me, Rob, and Amanda somewhere before or after. She had thrombocytopenia and had to receive platelets, as her platelets got really low before we knew she had this. She was bruising and had to be careful not to fall down and get hurt. She actually started bleeding in her mouth and Amanda knew something was bad wrong. We weren't sure what was happening with her and why she had this but it was about six months to a year that she had to deal with this. We prayed and believed for God to touch her and heal her and you know what? God did. It just went away, just like that, and we never did know why she had it but it was gone in Jesus' name, healed. I give God all the glory and praise for healing my beautiful granddaughter.

21

GREAT IS THY FAITHFULNESS O LORD

We stayed with our daughter and her family during the entire time of Rob's surgery and treatment. The timeframe was about six months. We still felt the call so strong that we are to go to Romania, but Rob was still not strong enough to be able to go for at least six months. I am calling out to God that I need a place to stay that we don't have to live with anyone. When we sold our home in February, we moved in with my parents and then after that with Amanda and her family. We were really needing a place of our own by now. I was like if we aren't going to Romania anytime soon then where *are* we going to live. We can't just keep on staying with relatives. We need a place of refuge and we cried out to the Lord.

He not only gave us a place to stay for 3 ½ months, but on a lake just down the road from my sister, Wanda's home. We kept the cutest little dog named Toby, a Boston Terrier. To stay at a lake home not only did we take care of Toby, but the owner also paid us to keep the dog. The home was very comfortable, it was beyond anything we could have done if we were looking for something like this ourselves. All we did was cry out to God and tell him our heart's desire and he showed up in a mighty way. Not only did we get to stay in a home on the lake, but neither of us worked. Every time I tried to look for something it was like God was saying to me why are you looking for work, this is your time to meditate on ME and seek my face for where I am taking you. God provided for our every little need. It was such a rewarding, relaxing time in our lives, after all we had been through finally rest.

Rob and I visited several churches and made many new friends. We felt we were to continue raising support for Romania as the call was even stronger than before and we had another date set for April 31, 2014 to leave for Romania. We started traveling some during this time but felt that South Carolina was the area we were to look for support. It seemed the harder we tried the less we could get into the churches, but then God worked it out for us to be on a Christian network, Nite-Line. Two and a half weeks before we were to leave to go back to Tennessee we were on Nite-Line out of Greenville, South Carolina. God opened the door for us to be in everyone's living room not just a few churches. We got the support we needed not necessarily through being on TV but enough to go to Romania. During the time we were in South Carolina, Rob went on Disability. He never got turned down, which the lawyer we had talked to said, 'It will take at least 18 months to maybe three years to get approved'; but not when God is in it. Wow Oh wow and he received the news on his birthday that the check would start the following Wednesday. So many blessings happened during this restful time in our lives.

22

DEBT PAID TO THE IRS

God had opened the door for us to develop property; Spring Creek Cove Subdivision. As we sold properties we began to acquire a large debt to the IRS. It was also during this time we got forgiveness of this debt of $39,000 from the IRS down to $1000.00, but God and only God could do this. We filed for a compromise and were told we would get denied. We didn't use a lawyer, although the lawyer I had talked to initially to find out about this compromise was very adamant that we would get denied and that I would need help to appeal. I thanked him and said I would contact the IRS myself.

I called the IRS and got the information I needed to file. We never got denied, it just happened and the way it happened just blew us away, very subtle just like, did this just happen? It had been very stressful dealing with the IRS and the pressure to pay this debt and that leans would be put against us if we went the route of not paying. No lean, no debt, forgiven, just forgiven. I stand in awe of HIM. I feel like the verse **Matthew 18.26-27 KJV 'The servant therefore fell down, and worshiped him, saying, "Lord, have patience with me, and I will pay thee all." Then the Lord of that servant was moved with compassion, and loosed him, and forgave him the debt.'** In all reality, this is what we had told the IRS, we wanted to pay our debt but needed to sell property to do so and could not continue to make payments with my husband's illness at this time. With that we were asked what could you pay and figuring we were stuck just said a $1000.00. When she said okay resend the compromise with that amount and you can take two years to pay this, just like that done. All in the name of Jesus. Cast all your cares on Him. **1 Peter 5.7 KJV 'Casting all your care upon him; for he careth for you'.** We literally put our total trust in Him, praying for favor, favor in our every aspect of our lives. This debt had accrued due to the development of Spring Creek Cove having to pay taxes up front for money we really hadn't made just the way it was set up and not fair to us but God made it fair, but God and only God. Wow, God!

Rob was recuperating and we were seeking God, getting ready to go to Romania as soon as God opened that door. He was preparing the way and as we stepped into His will on a daily basis, miracles were happening all around us. Cancer was not going to tell us we were not called to be missionaries. It was in our hearts so strong. We knew we were going to Romania with all that was in us. We continued to raise the support to go, faith rising up in us as we prepared our hearts and lifted God up and glorified Him for all He had done and was doing in our lives.

23

ANOTHER BUMP IN THE ROAD

We packed up and said goodbye to Toby and South Carolina, excited to go to Tennessee and see our kids and family. Rob was scheduled to get a CT scan for his three-month follow up. The CT showed an enlarged lymph node so a biopsy was done. The biopsy showed cancer back in the axillary region. This was some very disturbing news and our hearts just broke, as we know we heard God calling us and so we just continued to trust Him. Rob had been very encouraged that the biopsy would come back fine, as he believed we were going to Romania this time. When the news was the cancer was back for just a couple of minutes you could see such hurt in his face, but then he said. We are still going to Romania. He asked the oncologist, 'what if I do nothing and just go on and trust God. Dr. Anz said you might have a year if you do nothing but at least see about having it taken out. So, we ordered a PET scan to see if the cancer had spread anywhere else before we proceeded any further. Thank the Lord it was only in those lymph nodes so surgery was scheduled. The doctor who did the surgery didn't quite know how to take us. We told him we needed to get this done and be on our way to Romania. He said to us, you know he might have that drainage tube in for up to six weeks. He also said he should have more chemotherapy and radiation. His axillary system was removed with 17 nodes being positive for cancer out of 24. We didn't know how it was all going to happen but we felt so strong that we were going this time. As we cried out, 'Lord, we know we heard your call. We know you healed Rob but cancer again?'

Rob did so well after the surgery. He always got sick after surgery but this time he did not and even wanted something to eat. God touched him in a mighty way. At his two week checkup he still had the tube in and not looking like it was going to come out any time soon. The doctor released us as we said we were going to Romania with or without the drain. The doctor said he didn't recommend it but he could see we were determined and so we talked with him about our options over in Romania. I was apprehensive about going until the tube was out but Rob said we need to go now or we will never go. I was determined that we needed to wait, but then God spoke to me and said listen to your husband. I had all the excuses of why we should not go until it was out. We went to Romania three weeks later and Rob still had the drain tube in from the surgery. I can honestly say I had no fear of going once I surrendered it all to HIM, such a peace. We were finally on our way to Romania and only God opened the door, it was wide open and we took a giant step towards being in the perfect will of God.

We had been staying with my parents and had told them bye earlier before the cancer showed up on the test. We had gone down to Alabama to be with our daughter and her family during this time of getting tests done and not really talking about it to many people. Praying it would all go away and not be so and we would leave on time as scheduled. It was a teary moment with my parents. We were sad to say goodbye but then we came back for the three weeks after surgery for Rob to recuperate. We had a few more weeks with them and they will be forever cherished, as this would be the last time I would see my dad alive. Rob and I would sit and have coffee in the mornings with mom and dad, very special times to us. One morning as the day began mom and dad were busy with gardening and yard work as I saw my daddy on the lawnmower I said to Rob, 'I see my dad going away' and I cried not knowing the future but feeling like because we were leaving soon that that was it. The day we left was on a Sunday to go to Alabama a few days and then we were flying out of Atlanta on Tuesday. As we said our final goodbyes this time I felt so strong about daddy. I just said to him, 'daddy don't die while I am gone'. Still I was thinking I was feeling this way because we would be gone for seven months across the world. We left and were really on our way this time.

24

ROMANIA BOUND

We arrived in Hungary on May 21st after a two day trip across the ocean. Rob had no trouble getting through the airport with the drain in; something I was concerned about, but God took such good care of us. The excitement we felt that we were finally on our way even with all we had just been through was so amazing. It was God's will for us to go and He made the way and said go and go now and trust Me and we did. We trust God with our whole life and only want to please the Lord.

Simona and John Sas came over from Oradea, Romania to pick us up. It is about a three hour drive one way. This was the first time meeting them. During the drive to Oradea we enjoyed getting to know them. Thank the Lord they spoke English, a precious couple that loves the Lord. Simona is the secretary at the Chaplaincy Center where we would be staying. We have come to love this couple so very much. They have two children, Mattie and Clarrisa. Vasile, who is Simona's stepdad, also works at the Center as the Custodian. When we got to the Care Center, Felicia Costea had made us a delicious meal. It was so good to be able to have a hot meal waiting on us. We had met Felicia Costea and her husband, Iulian ,about two years earlier when we started making our plans to go to Romania. They are Romanian but had been in the United States ten years and were now at the center as missionaries and we were coming to help and assist them, or so we thought at the time.

We got settled in on the top floor of the Care Center in Oradea. We needed a refrigerator to have everything we needed to set up house and so we went and bought one. The apartment has two bedrooms, two baths, a kitchen with a long hallway type living area that goes out onto a very large terrace overlooking Oradea. Rob and I enjoyed our coffee time out there lots of mornings and some evenings we would have our supper there. It was an adjustment. We were right next to the Penny market and the outdoor market. We could walk to the mall in 20 minutes, which we did a lot of walking. It is quite nice and we enjoyed shopping there, lots of restaurants and a big grocery store that had all we could want.

Shortly after we got to Romania Rob's mom had to be hospitalized. We prayed God would touch her and she got better. We didn't know if we might have to go home as it was pretty serious. Then a couple of weeks after that my daddy got sick and was really very sick. This confirmed the urgency we had to go when we did with Rob having the drain in as had we waited another two weeks daddy would have gotten sick and I don't think I would have been able to leave him. We would Skype daddy often. He loved it and thought it was the neatest thing to be able to see each other across the world. They tried to keep it from us as long as they could that daddy was sick, as everyone knew the struggles we had had to get to Romania. Daddy did not want us to come home, but my heart was there and it was also in Romania where we knew God wanted us.

I had a separation anxiety attack one morning after we first got to Romania. I think knowing I was going to be there for seven months and away from our kids and family and in a foreign country. Rob helped me, prayed with me and I adjusted quickly. There were only bunk beds in the rooms but after a couple of weeks Rob figured out how to make us a big bed by putting two of the bunk beds together and building a frame. In Europe, all the beds are low to the ground so he got us back up to where we are used to sleeping and it was quite nice. There was also an air conditioner that worked that all it needed was to be set up with a tube out the window. He got that fixed up for us with Vasile. Now I was feeling a little spoiled. We had air conditioning at night and that made it nice because the mosquitoes were eating us up with the windows opened, which had no screens. Those first few days were an adjustment as I had no blow-dryer or curling iron so I had to purchase those things. It was great to have a washing machine and an iron, although I had to dry the clothes on the terrace air dry, that worked but a lot different than what I am used to. You don't see dryers, but they do have them with the washing machines, just most people hang their clothes out to dry.

Romania – Oradea Chaplaincy

We went to church that first Sunday with Simona and John. It was so different from how we worship but the same in that I felt the Holy Spirit. The ladies all wear scarfs on their heads. No pants or jewelry. The women and men sit separate. Of course everything was in Romanian except when Rob spoke and he did speak several times, testifying and then preach some while in Oradea and some surrounding villages.

Iulian introduced us to Sam who works with one of the Children's orphanages. We were not sure what we would be doing but knew it would be with children, so we wanted to start there. Simona helped us with learning the Romanian language and we also got into a free class for about two months twice a week. So we learned some but there are a lot of people that speak English so it is easy to communicate with the Romanians; actually I am finding out that English is spoken all over the world, it is the language that everyone wants to speak.

Iulian and Felicia shared with us that they would be leaving to go back to the states. They felt like their time there was coming to an end and felt they were to go to Chicago to pastor a church there. It had taken us longer to get there due to Rob's illness and so we were disappointed that they would be leaving. They left about two weeks after we arrived and it made us sad to see them go, but we knew God always has a plan. We really did not know what we would be doing since everything was changing with the chaplaincy. We were ready to do ministry, but we would have to find out what that ministry was. We felt like God had sent us here for such a time as this. Simona and the staff looked to us and maybe we were there for them as the changes took place. We were not in charge but we could pray and seek the Lord and assist in anyway God showed us. There were some stressful times for the center and not knowing what was going on ourselves. We would just pray and trust the Lord that all things will work out for His glory.

25

GOD HAS GOT YOUR BACK

We finally got involved with Simona's church, teaching a vacation Bible school in a village that was an hour away. The pastor came one day and talked to us about several ideas he had and one was to do this bible school.

It took several weeks as we had to plan accordingly with the lady at the church in the village where we would have the bible school. It was so exciting to plan the lessons and crafts. We could feel that this was something in our hearts that we wanted to be a part of and would put our whole heart into it. Simona's grandfather lived near that village and we got to meet him and also an aunt who fixed us a couple of meals as we picked up some children there. They made us feel so welcomed and the food was so delicious.

During this time, my dad was getting worse and it wasn't looking so good. I would say daddy I will come home and he would say 'No, I will be here in December when you get home'. We felt we were to stay and so we continued to do work in Romania as we prayed for my daddy to be healed. It was hard at times but God helped us to have peace. One Sunday Rob and I wanted to go to the Charismatic church in Oradea to see if they worshiped more like what we are used to. The music was good and everyone could sit together and raise their hands in worship. It was all in Romanian but something amazing happened. When the pastor was exhorting the congregation he said the words, 'God has got your back' in English. I was looking for the scripture in my bible when he said this and I said to Rob, 'Did he just say God has got your back in English?' And Rob says, 'Yes'. We didn't realize it was a direct message from the Lord until that evening when we got word that daddy was worse and we needed to come home now. God had not released us to go yet, it would be another two weeks and some of my family did not understand why we didn't just get on a plane and come on home right then. When you are in the will of the Lord, he reveals to you as you follow Him and he had not revealed to us we were to go home yet. We were still believing God would heal daddy and so those words were very comforting to us in more ways than one to come to us during this time. We were so involved in the bible school and were hoping to do another one that we just couldn't feel we were to leave. We had just found what we felt in our hearts to be where God was leading us.

26

TIME TO GO HOME

We had been staying in the Terrace apartment and some other missionary friends were coming back from where they had been staying and would need a place to live also. We were asked to move into the apartment where Iulian and Felicia had stayed. The missionaries that originally had been at the Center before would be coming back and we would share the apartment with them for a short while. We had hoped that we could have stayed in the Terrace apartment as we loved the Terrace, but we moved graciously. We were feeling a little bit like we were in the way and I was now feeling like I wanted to go home to the states. My daddy was sick and dying. We felt at this time God had released us to go. I had not felt like this and the release was coming. I have found that when you let the Lord lead you he will tell you the plans but sometimes not until the last moment so we have to stay in tune to His voice. It took some time to get our plane tickets to get home so my daddy passed away before I could get there. I felt all along I would not be there when he passed. It was like God gave me a prophetic word before I left. The last goodbye to my daddy was, 'Daddy don't die while I am gone'. He wasn't even sick but I felt this so strong. I took comfort in knowing it was okay that I wasn't there, as God had revealed this to me. I knew he had passed before I even got home and had mourned him all the way home. My family had expected me to be upset, but I had such a peace that only God can give.

It would have been easy to have not gone back to Romania, as I had felt the doors had closed in Oradea with the other missionaries coming back, but our daughter, Amanda, said she felt like we were to go back, so she booked a return ticket back to Oradea. Our plans were to stay until the middle of December. I said we can stay home but when God books your tickets, as it would have been very easy for her to say maybe you should stay home as her dad (Rob) needed to be followed up by a doctor every three months, but he had chosen to wait seven months and still chose to wait as Rob was feeling fine and wanted to get back to Romania. There was a work that we still needed to find, as we had not found it yet and being home in the states made us realize we had to go back. We stayed 30 days in the states and then went back to Romania for three more months.

27

MEDGIDIA, ROMANIA

When we arrived back in Oradea, we both felt this is so right. It felt so good to be back, but then it was like this isn't it. We were no longer doing the bible schools and we were sharing the apartment with Caroline the missionary that had come to run the Center. It was awkward at first but we managed. We visited with Caroline a bible study with some people from the states and enjoyed the fellowship with other English speaking people and some Romanians that also spoke English, but still we did not feel this was the place. One Saturday morning, Rob and I decided to make up twelve lunches and wrote John 3.16 and 'Jesus Loves You' in Romanian and went to a couple of parks to witness and share Jesus. There was one man who we woke up and as we gave him the lunch and shared Jesus he just cried. It was a touching moment and maybe he was the one we were to encourage that day, as the rest just seemed to take it and go. Also, while in Oradea we had met this Hungarian missionary and he had taken us out to a couple of villages where we took some food and shoes to a couple of families. We checked on this one girl and her baby at least three times. We just wanted to go out into all the world and share the love of Jesus and as God opened the doors we followed. We still didn't feel like this was where we were supposed to be, so as we cried out to the Lord he directed us in another direction.

The Lord directed us to Medgidia, Romania. We had wanted to visit some castles while in Romania and so we made plans with another missionary family to go to Brosov and visit two castles, Peles and the Branz Castle know as Dracula's Castle. They had been down in Medgidia and as we shared our heart with them, they said you need to go on down to Medgidia and see all the work with the gypsies and the children there. Our heart had been with the children and felt that was the call with the children. So, we packed extra clothes and decided since we weren't too far away that we should check out Medgidia.

Medgidia, Romania

When we got there I did not like it, very poor and I just could feel all the evil there, a lot of Muslim, orthodox, and satanic forces. I told Rob no I don't want to stay here after our friends left. He said let's just give it a little more time and if we still don't feel this is where God wants us then we will go back to Oradea in a few days. The very next week there was a Women's Conference scheduled to take place in Bethlehem church and to go to all the other village churches associated with this ministry as well. There were six women who came in from England and a couple of ladies from the states. Cindy had asked me if I would be interested in decorating and cooking the breakfast that first day of the conference for the pastors wives, and before I knew it I was so busy that at the end of that week I told Rob we are to stay and of course he agreed.

So, we set out to work as hard as we could and helped with the Care Center cooking, teaching bible stories, helping with homework, teaching songs, decorating for Christmas, going to buy Christmas presents for the kids. We were so busy it was great. I had said I want to work like 9 to 5 every day and be busy as if I were working a job. Be careful what you ask for because we were so busy, it was a good busy, very rewarding. We made many friends and met several people from other countries. It was a great two months.

Medgidia Community Center

We even got to go and be part of an Encounter Conference in Bucharest that was two hours away. I had been in charge of fixing them breakfast and was glad to share with them, not thinking anything about going. Right before they left, Vasi came up to me and said they had room for two more if Rob and I wanted to go. We literally had five minutes to pack. I have never packed that fast in my life, it was such a great feeling to just go and be a part of something that I didn't plan for. We found out that even on the mission field God still pours into you, encouraging and lifting you up in the midst of all the work we were involved in. God has little nuggets for us along the way. When we least expect it, he shows up with a time of refreshing. It was a great time spent in the Lord with prayer and just being with other brothers and sisters in Christ. It doesn't matter what nationality you are when you meet a fellow Christian you find you are connected. We are all the same in the eyes of Christ. The people who spoke at the Encounter were from England; it seems we have met so many people from England in the short time we were in Romania. It was a good break from Medgidia and so refreshing to get away.

Rob had been doing some sheet-rock sanding and one evening he started hurting in his face. He stayed in bed for a whole day with this pain. I was concerned but he didn't want me to call Amanda to talk with her about it, but finally in the middle of the night he woke me up. He said to me, 'Cheryl this pain is not going to stop. We are going to have to go home.' I was feeling a little scared at that moment not sure what might be going on with him. So I called Amanda trying not to sound so scared but I just wanted to cry when I heard her voice, but I didn't want to upset her so I was able to keep my composure. I think just calling her in the middle of our night was scary enough for her. Amanda said to start an antibiotic and to take more Ibuprofen. He was feeling sick so we waited until morning on the antibiotic but I prayed for him for three hours and just kept saying 'Jesus, Jesus'. Every time I would almost go off to sleep he would seem like he would hurt but as long as I spoke the name of Jesus and prayed over him he continued to get better. By morning, the pain eased off and never did return. We didn't even consider going back early after that. He was up and ready to go by morning. It was evident that God had touched him. We started the antibiotics, but he was already feeling so much better before the medicine even had a chance to work. We still had another month before we were to go back to the United States. We felt so strong that we were to stay until December 16th as planned originally.

Snow in Medgidia

We got involved with the Christmas shopping for the kids and wrapping Christmas presents and decorating the trees. I love to decorate at Christmas time and especially the tree. I have several ornaments that I have made through the years and it is a nostalgic time putting up the tree and remembering Christmases past. We had sold our artificial Christmas tree before we left in May. Rob and I usually enjoyed going to the Christmas tree farm and picking out a real tree anyway so why keep it. It was a tradition that we both loved. We had purchased an artificial tree a few years back during the time we were building and selling homes to decorate for an open house. I think I secretly wanted an artificial tree so I could decorate earlier but I still love the real trees and the excitement of picking it out together. We would take grandkids sometimes and our kids when they were at home, but if it was just him and I it was just as fun.

Manta, who stayed at the center, helped me with the decorations. He grew up in an Orphanage and through Cindy he made his way to Medgidia. He lives at the center and is one of the Team members. We stayed at the center for the two months we were in Medgidia. Our room was right next to Manta's. One Friday night, around 10.30 or 11.00 all of a sudden our bed started moving. I said to Rob, 'Manta is having a party or something in his room. He needs to settle down.' When I checked on what was going on with him we found out we just had an earthquake. We laugh about it now. In all reality there was no way he could have made the bed move anyway if he was having a party, what was I thinking.

I always love to make Christmas cookies with the grandkids during Christmas so I decided to make cookies for the kids at the Center to decorate and eat. We made four recipes of Christmas cookies. It was a lot of fun making these cookies. Rob enjoyed helping me cut them out. The kids enjoyed putting icing on them and then eating them. We gave them milk to drink with their cookies, it was really a treat for them.

28

THY WILL BE DONE

We were about a week out before we would be leaving to go on the long train ride back to Oradea and then make our way to Hungary to fly back to the United States as our time here in Romania was coming to an end. Rob started getting some pain and swelling in his arm. I was a little concerned, but was hoping it was due to him over-using the arm. He was very active and there was no telling him to slow down. He loved every minute he was there with the kids in Romania. We set down with Vasi and Cindy and discussed coming back in March 2015. We were presented with a proposition if we wanted to head up the project for Tortoman. The plans are to start up another program like the one in Medgidia in the Tortoman church. The kids are brought from Tortoman to Medgidia. When the program can start in Tortoman then the kids would not have to be picked up and brought to Medgidia and more children can be in the Program in Tortoman and Medgidia. We were told how much they needed to do the renovations and make the church bigger. The amount estimated that would be needed was $15,000.00. We didn't hesitate to reply with, 'We would be happy to head up this project feeling in hearts that this was God's plan'. Trusting that whatever happens, His will would be done.

As we headed on the train to Oradea Rob's arm continued to hurt and swell even more. We rubbed it and prayed for it and wrapped it treating it like lymph edema, because that is what can happen if you over use the arm when you have no lymph nodes. We got to Oradea and had a week before flying home. We enjoyed some time with Simona and John and said goodbye to them. It was sad as when we were going to come back it would be to Medgidia and not Oradea and we really loved them and were sad that we could not work in Oradea, but God has given us the heart for Medgidia and apparently the door for Oradea had closed, or so it seemed.

Tortoman Church

It was a long wait in the airport. We were just ready to get home and had decided due to so much luggage and Rob in a lot of pain to just stay at the airport. I couldn't lift the luggage and neither could Rob so instead of spending the night in a hotel we elected to wait at the airport. It was a long painful night for Rob. I don't think either one of us was thinking straight and having the driver drop us off at a hotel and catch a shuttle in the morning would have been the smart thing to do. After the 12 hour plane ride back to the states we were finally home. It was so good to be back in the states, but reality had set in.

Rob continued to get worse with pain and at his oncology appointment on December 24th, after a CAT scan, it was confirmed that the cancer was back and in his brachial plexus nerve, and that was what was causing all the pain and swelling. It was very upsetting news, but we still believed that God was going to raise Rob up. It was the hardest Christmas I have ever faced in my life. My heart was so heavy and I prayed and cried and cried and prayed some more. I can honestly say I had peace, but my joy left that day. We started down this road again, but no more surgery could be done. Rob had to be started on pain medicines which he was not crazy about, but as it helped his pain he would agree to take it, but not as much as he needed or as often as he should until he just couldn't bear it anymore. He started radiation and chemotherapy the middle of January, it seemed because of the holidays that it was hard to get anything any sooner and he was in so much pain that it was just very frustrating. They were able to regulate his pain better with extended release pain Meds and more milligrams.

The weekend after Rob's first chemotherapy and radiation treatments I took a trip to Tennessee to speak at Community Hall Church in Cleveland, Tennessee. I didn't want to go at first and leave him but he encouraged me to go, that I could do it. I don't consider myself a speaker, but God opened the door and I felt like I had to go and share what God was doing in our lives, and to ask and believe for Rob's healing. I enjoyed sharing what God was doing in Romania. I was so excited to share that it just consumed me. I had never experienced being in front of a crowd speaking quite like this before and to know the joy that I was sharing from my heart and what God wanted me to share. I usually will sing and play the piano and testify, but speaking was new to me.

By this time, just by word of mouth and sharing about raising money for the Tortoman Project, it just happened. Our home church, Woodward Avenue Church of God took this on and $10,000 above what was needed was raised. Here we are, dealing with Rob's illness, and not really sure how we are going to be able to raise this and it just happened. We had no doubt that we could raise it when we said we would, but when we got back home and Rob's cancer was back my first thought was, 'How are we going to raise this money now we can't focus on going to churches to raise it', but God had a plan and His plan was far beyond anything we ever could have ever imagined. I must say it blew us away to see God move in a mighty way and be a part of what God is doing in Medgidia, Romania. All we have to do is obey and sow the seed and He will do the rest. We just have to serve Him and make known our request.

29

KEEPING THE FAITH

At the end of Rob's treatment in March he seemed to be better by about 20 percent, so we decided to take a trip to Tennessee. He was getting out and walking and doing more than he was. He seemed to be feeling a lot better. My dad's sister had passed away and mom didn't want to go alone. Rob had said you need to take your mom I will be alright here alone. So I decided to take mom to Savannah, Georgia. He was speaking that following Sunday morning at Community Hall Church. I hated to miss being there when he spoke, but I felt at peace to go. He was even able to drive himself with the car and he had not been driving any before this. I must say I wasn't crazy about leaving him. He did quite well and it was encouraging to us both. His arm seemed to be some better, but that only lasted for a short time.

We had been invited to go with the Keenagers at our church for a weekend get-away at the Moose Lodge in Gatlinburg, Tennessee. It was so nice to be with our church family. The place was really nice and had lots of rooms and a great big kitchen and open area for lots of people to be together playing games, eating, and socializing. The view was absolutely amazing to just sit and gaze at God's beauty. The sun was out nice and the sky was clear on that Saturday and we just had a wonderful time. Rob's arm started swelling again and we would rub it and try to get the swelling to go down. It would make his arm feel better, but it would swell right back up again. I was feeling a little concerned but just prayed and kept believing for the miracle. We love the outdoors and hiking and so we were able to take a short walk around the place. Rob seemed to start to go downhill again during this trip, and all I could do was be there for him and just pray and believe. It was so hard to see him in so much pain. He was on pain Meds but he was careful not to take too much, not wanting to get addicted to pain Meds.

When we were heading back to Alabama after our weekend trip to Gatlinburg. We decided to stop at a Western Sizzlin to eat in Fort Payne, Alabama. I noticed Rob was struggling even more. He didn't want me to know and was good to be strong, but I knew and I hurt for him. We got in the car and were heading on down the road when all of a sudden I noticed his wedding band was missing off his finger. He had no clue when it may have fallen off. I thought maybe at the steakhouse or possibly the Moose Lodge, but we didn't go back or call and check at either place. We just knew it was gone. At that moment, we both just started crying. I think that is when it really hit us that he was going to die. I cried for the rest of that trip and he did too. It was a hard day and a feeling I won't ever forget. This journey was not one I wanted to be on, but I do know that God was with us and He held our hand and was always right there with us. The tears were somehow soothing to my heart because as I am crying, I am crying out to God from the bottom of my heart and He knows. We continued to pray and believe for God to raise Rob up and give him more years on this earth to continue the work that we felt so strong that God had opened that door.

During all of this, God was moving on our finances. We still had five lots in Spring Creek Cove that we needed to sell and God was working on making that happen. We had a closing setup in Athens on one of the lots and so we took another trip to Tennessee. Rob had started getting redness and burning under his arm so we started putting creams under his arm and he started taking an antibiotic. He decided he could make the trip and so we went. It was a painful trip. He pushed himself to go and that evening after the closing he wanted to go the Emergency Room as he was taking a turn for the worse. They admitted him at Memorial Hospital in Chattanooga, Tennessee. They did chest x-rays and blood tests and encouraged us that they didn't see more cancer. Several people from Restoration Church came and prayed for Rob and it was a great time in the Lord, speaking positive over him and the situation. Several family members came and just set with us and encouraged us. He was able to go home after a few days. So we headed back to Alabama, since it was more comfortable there and was where we were staying during this time.

We weren't back a week when all of a sudden while I was out shopping with Addie, my granddaughter, that something strange happened with Rob that he couldn't seem to get something out of his throat. He lost his voice and could not talk anymore because of this. Amanda was there and said it was a little scary when it happened for him, but he was okay and that we probably should take him to get checked out. We decided on going to the hospital ER in Prattville, Alabama. They ended up admitting him, come to find out he had a blood clot in his arm, which I am not sure why that wasn't detected before in Chattanooga, unless maybe it developed since the weekend.

I know he had been in a lot of pain and that explained all the pain. They did an x-ray and confirmed radiation damage had caused the diaphragm to push up against his voice box causing him to not be able to talk. He eventually was able to talk later some better as his body re-trained to talk from the other side of his lung but never normal again. He was in the hospital for several days and started on a blood thinner. This was when he started spiraling downhill. I would stay with him all night and day and then in the afternoons I would go home and shower and take a walk to clear my head and pray. During my walks, I would just weep and cry from the bottom of my heart out to God and look up to heaven. A couple of times, there would be colors of rainbows in the clouds with the sun shinning. I felt like God was saying to me I am here with you and I know your pain and to just trust Me. I will never leave you or forsake you. **Deuteronomy 31.6 KJV 'Be strong and courageous. Do not be afraid or terrified because of them, for the Lord your God goes with you, he will never leave you nor forsake you'.** In my case I was afraid of the cancer and the situation. It was comforting to look and see this. It was beautiful. I just love how God speaks to us when we reach out in need. He is always right there. I must say I felt God with me every step of this journey. I cried a lot but it was a soothing cry to my spirit. I literally felt what I call God hugging me during this time. It is just the only way I can explain how He held me in his hands.

Rob needed to get his arm moving again and so he was able to start some physical therapy, just some range of motion movement, but not any pressing or massaging with the blood clot present. It seemed good to get the approval to start something on trying to improve his arm. He worked diligently, trying to work that arm. It was so painful for him. It hurt me to see him in so much pain but the physical therapist was encouraging that it would be painful, but that is how it works to get the arm loosened up. He endured the pain and was a soldier in trying so hard.

30

TIME TO GO HOME TO TENNESSEE

Shortly after starting physical therapy it was time for his follow up PET scan to see where he was with everything. It wasn't a good report, not at all what we were expecting or believing for. The cancer had spread and had shown that it was in the area of the radiation burn that was constantly getting worse. Dr. Davidson said he could give Rob more chemotherapy to help beat the cancer back some and could buy more time, but Rob chose to do nothing else. He didn't want to do something that was going to make him feel bad and would not cure him. He said the cancer wasn't in a vital organ so he really didn't know how long he would live. We told Dr. Davidson we were believing for the miracle of God to raise him up, and if God chose the ultimate healing then either way Rob would be healed and we thanked him for all he did for him and us.

Rob decided that he wanted to go back to Athens to die. If God was going to take him to Heaven and he receive the ultimate healing, then he wanted to tell anyone and everyone he knew bye. He wanted to make sure that they were ready to go to Heaven. It was a very sad time. He spoke into Timothy and Addie and Amanda and Peter. My heart was breaking and nothing I could do would change the situation. I believed with my whole heart for God to heal him, but the healing wasn't going to come the way I wanted it. When I think back, we prayed for God to get the most glory in His healing, and if taking Rob to Heaven was the most, then I would have to accept it. I would say surely God you would be glorified more by healing Rob on this side of Heaven, but in my heart I was feeling something different. I still hung on until the last moment that maybe just maybe God would give us more time together to do the work that He showed us. I do know God gave me so much strength. It was the hardest thing I have ever had to do to watch such a strong man die and the love of my life. He wanted to go to mom's to die. I wasn't so sure that that would be a good idea, but mom opened her door for us to come. There was a struggle there that I am not sure I understand what was happening. It seemed the more I believed the harder I felt attacked, like I was supposed to just give up on him. When we first got to mom's, Rob was depressed and he could have very easily died the first of June. He was able to go upstairs and sleep the first few days, one night he fell in the bathroom. At first it was scary and then funny and then we both cried. He said, 'I am going away'. He had given up the will to live and fight anymore.

31

YOU WILL LIVE AND NOT DIE

We had a get-to-gather with the Wilson clan the first weekend back home at mom's. It was a sad time, but a precious time to just hug on Rob and Rob hug on them and everyone tell him and he them how much they loved him and he loved them. So many people came by to visit and he witnessed to the ones he wanted to make sure were saved. He didn't let cancer dictate to him. He was in a lot of pain but we were able to regulate his pain for him to go to church, out to eat a time or two. He was put on Hospice. One afternoon some friends came by with an encouraging word. The word was from **Psalm 117.18 KJV 'You will live and not die and proclaim all that the Lord has done'.** We started standing on this promise and speaking healing over Rob.

This was when the struggle started. We were believing for this miracle on this side of Heaven. We had a prayer time and fasting one evening and anyone who wanted to come that believed for his healing to come and pray with us. I would not give up on Rob and because of that I believe Rob had six more weeks of quality time with family and friends. He even said to me that it was because of my faith that he was better, and he really seemed like he was getting better. Several people would come and pray the prayer of faith over him and it encouraged both of us that he was going to live and not die. I am so thankful for people who will take a stand for the Lord and pray for people to be healed and speak life over the situation and the person and families who are needing the prayer warriors to intercede on their behalf. We do have life eternally with God. We will never die, our spirit lives on forever and ever. How we are to spend eternity is up to us. We have that choice. We can chose life or we can chose death. It is God's desire for us to live for Him and love Him back. He loved us so much that He sent His son to die for us so that we can have eternal life. He is sad when we don't choose to follow Him.

I have never seen anything like this. The cancer was coming out in sores under his arm and neck. It originally had started with a cellulitis burn from radiation. We prayed for the cancer to get out of his body to come out and so it appeared it was. I stayed positive and wouldn't see any negative. I believed the sores were getting better even though they had started spreading and bleeding more. Sometimes when I would change his dressings it would just overwhelm me so much that I would just cry, they would bleed and it was scary at times. I enjoyed taking care of him. I wanted to take his pain away and I would just pray God help us, give us strength and He did. A strength that was supernatural and came from God my Heavenly Father. I know He literally held me up so I could hold up my husband. It was not in my own strength.

Rob would get up every morning and have coffee and breakfast and sit in the sun-room or outside. He never laid in bed. He wanted to be awake and visit any and all who would come. He had such dignity through all of this. Cancer is a horrible disease, but he did not let it take him out without a fight and being even more of a witness through his illness. So many people's lives were touched. He wanted to make sure everyone was saved because he was going to Heaven soon and he wanted to make sure he would see you again, and the only way for that to happen was to ask Jesus into your heart and be forgiven of all your sins. **Romans 10.9-10 that if you confess with your mouth the Lord**

Jesus and believe in your heart that God has raised Him from the dead, you will be saved. For with the heart one believes unto righteousness, and with the mouth confession is made unto salvation. Romans 10.13 'For whoever calls on the name of the Lord shall be saved'.

He was so worried about his brother, like himself he works so hard and barely has time for his family. He never went to church and going to church doesn't save you, but when you are saved the scripture says in **Hebrews 10.25 'Not forsaking the assembling of ourselves together, as the manner of some is; but exhorting one another: and so much the more, as ye see the day approaching'.** I am so thankful for our church family. We have to lift each other up and encourage one another. He wanted that for his brother and most of all that he would come to know Jesus as his personal savior. It was a sad time, but also a precious time to see the love between him and his brother. During the last six weeks of Rob's life his brother went to a church with him a couple of times. Rob encouraged him to get connected with a church and went with him to a church he agreed to go to in Etowah. He was weak but he went, it was great to be with his brother and his family with him in church. It meant a lot to Rob, and another miracle that Rob witnessed in his last days. It was amazing to see such strength in Rob, he was even able to go out to eat once after church with his brother and his family. We were believing God was healing him on this side of Heaven, but our prayer was for God to be glorified in all of this. I sometimes would say to God, 'Healing Rob on this side wouldn't that be more glory for you Lord', but in my heart I knew the answer, but I continued to believe and ask and praise the Lord for whatever the decision would be. It didn't change my faith in God because I trust God and I know His plans are far beyond anything I could ever hope for or imagine. **Isaiah 55.9 'For as the Heavens are higher than the earth, so are my ways higher than your ways, and my thoughts than your thoughts'.** God was omnipresent, ever present, every moment. He was always there with us through every step of the way. **Psalm 46.1 'God is our refuge and strength, a very present help in trouble'**, and was He ever present. My strength came from Him. He literally held me up. I could not hold myself up. **Psalm 28.7 'The Lord is my strength and my shield; my heart trusts in Him, and He helps me. My heart leaps for joy; and with my song I praise him.'** He is the source of my strength. He is the strength of my life.

Rob would get up most mornings around 5.00 a.m. and pray for others as God revealed to him who to pray for. It was a special time for him. One morning I was concerned about letting him get up and pray by himself and so I got up and set in the sun-room with him. He told me he would be alright, but I was stubborn this one morning as he had just fell a few days before. I was worried about him falling so I got up, but complaining that I was tired and I needed him to stay in bed a little while longer. As I listened to him pray it was so beautiful. It wasn't about God heal him. He prayed for any and everyone, people that were sick, people that he just felt like God wanted him to pray for. He prayed for me, prayed for his children and grandchildren, my mom, my siblings, his siblings, parents, relatives, friends, people he didn't even really know. Here is a man who was sick and barely able to do for himself but was pushing himself every morning to get up and spend time with the Lord in prayer, but not selfishly praying for himself but for others. One morning he came into the bedroom after he had been up for a while praying and said, 'Cheryl I need to tell you what God told me this morning'. He said whenever you get up, well of course I was ready, I wanted to hear what God had spoke to him. He said as he was praying this morning God asked him,' If I don't heal you are you going to still serve Me,' and he said, 'Yes Lord, I will always serve you and love you'. He then told Rob as he works his arm up towards Heaven he would be totally healed. I think it was at this moment I realized God was taking him home. I said to Rob, so put your arm up to Heaven just do it and you will be healed. Rob said, I have to work it up that way. He showed me and tried, but it wouldn't go very far, but he was very adamant that He would be healed. I know God was talking to him and preparing to take him home. I needed to prepare but I was still holding on for healing on this side and encouraged him all the more that he would live and not die and proclaim all that the Lord has done.

32

THE FACE OF JESUS

Another time we were sitting outside and he had his shirt off and I noticed some red bruised like areas on his back. I was looking at them and all of a sudden I realized he had a face on his back. I took a picture so he could see it. I felt comforted by this face. I knew Jesus was taking care of him and all I needed to do was trust in Jesus. **Proverbs 3.5 'Trust in the Lord with all your heart and lean not on your own understanding'.** I can't explain the face, it looked like Jesus.

Many times as I cried out to God for help for comfort for why, what, please help me Lord, help us Lord. I don't want to do this anymore, can't we just be healed and proclaim what the Lord is doing and has done, and we did. In the midst of this time in our lives we continued to glorify God. The Lord always gave me something to help me through each moment and day and time. I call them 'little nuggets of encouragement during this time' I grasped hold of every positive that I could. There was no room for negative talk, I wouldn't allow it and sometimes I felt like I had no support in believing for Rob to be healed. I wouldn't look at the circumstance because like it says in **Hebrews 11.1 'Faith is the substance of things hoped for the evidence of things not seen'.** I have seen God move in my life and I knew He was moving and I trust in Him. He was carrying me as I was just surviving in the Savior's arms. My heart was in tune with him. He was taking me places with Him that no one knew but me and God. We serve an awesome God. He is with us every step of the way in the midst of pain and sorry. **Deuteronomy 31.8 'The Lord Himself goes before you and will be with you. He will never leave you nor forsake you. Do not be afraid. Do not be discouraged.'**

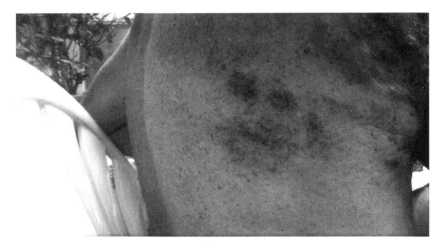

The Face of Jesus

33

THE LAST TIME

On July 4th weekend, we met our daughter and her family over in Cloudland Canyon. This would be the last time we would get to have a get away in the mountains with our children and grandchildren. My heart was breaking to see him so sick, and I believed with my whole heart that he was going to get well and be made whole on this side of heaven. As I look back now I see how God held me in his hand as I walked out every day crying out to God and looking to him for strength and guidance, trusting that He knows what is best for us. We prayed that God would be glorified in all of this. Lots of times I would pray and say things to God like, healing Rob on this side, 'wouldn't YOU God be glorified more', maybe if we prayed no matter what heal Rob on this side. We were all about God getting the most glory in all of this. I know I had so much peace through this time. I cried lots of tears and we cried lots of tears together. We were standing on faith and believing he would live and not die.

It was a relaxing time and much needed time to spend together. He loved his family and cherished all the times we spent with our son and his family and our daughter and her family. We couldn't always get all of us together and had hoped to get everyone together this time, but we were staying positive. So we didn't say this could be the last time with your dad, maybe that thought entered my mind, but I would not entertain it. I stayed positive and my son believed his dad was going to be around for a lot longer. He tells me now, 'I know dad was terminal and it was bad, but I was believing for the miracle. I never really thought he was going to die.'

I would always encourage and say things to my children, 'I believe in miracles, I believe God is healing your dad. I am standing on the word of God and the word does not lie.' We never did demand that God just heal Rob. We stood on the word and promises of God and asked for more time, but we always wanted God to get the most glory out of all of this and that was Rob's desire. Sometimes I wish I would have been more selfish and just said heal him no matter, but would that be right to take the glory away from God? Because I really believe he would have been healed on this side if we had approached it in a selfish way, but how much glory would God have gotten. I feel so many people were touched by the faith that we both showed and proclaimed even though it didn't turn out the way I had hoped, it turned out the way God planned it to be. I can tell you more people were touched in his death of the faith and peace that we both experienced during this time.

34

IN THE VALLEY OF THE SHADOW OF DEATH

Over the next two weeks Rob started declining, having lots of phlegm coming up, his arm was draining a lot of fluid and I was having to change it to keep it dry several times a day. The sores were bleeding a lot and looked to be spreading over to the other side of his neck. It was unlike anything I would have ever imagined. I kept them as clean as I could, as there would be an odor coming from them. He was able to get in the shower and never did get bedridden until two days before he died. He fought hard to the end to live. You know going to heaven is going to be beautiful when it is our time to go. We fight to live because it is in us to live. God made us that way, but when it is our time he gets us ready. I know now that Rob hung on because of me. I was fighting so hard to keep him here. I wanted us to grow old together, to go back and work side by side on the mission field. We were so good together. We completed each other. He seemed to be getting weaker, but he still would get up out of bed early every morning and spend time with God and just enjoy the day with family and friends.

We had called in Hospice and had planned for him to die at my mother's home. On the Sunday before his death he started feeling like his heart was racing and having symptoms that warranted calling an ambulance. Being in Hospice I called them and told them and they said give him more morphine, now Rob did not want to be knocked out. He wanted to fight and live and not die. So we pulled Hospice and called the ambulance and he went to the Emergency Room. They gave him some IV fluids, he was getting dehydrated from all the fluid he was losing. I don't think we realized he wasn't drinking as much as his body was excreting. He felt so much better. The doctor decided to send him home because of the sores on his body it would be better not to stay in the hospital because of high risk of infection with the opened sores. I had called Amanda earlier in the day asking her what should we do. She had drove over from Alabama and got to the house just as we were getting back from the Emergency Room. Rob rested really good that night and we were encouraged that he was going to get better. Amanda stayed around until about 4.00 p.m.

The next day, Rob had started having problems getting fluids like milk shakes and Ensure to go down. He kept saying it was not going down. I tried and tried to get him to drink telling him you have to drink. Hospice had come and got the oxygen and all of the things we had to help him since we pulled Hospice. He was needing oxygen. He started acting like he was out of it so instead of calling an ambulance his sister, Karen came over and helped me get him in the car. He was able to walk but it was a struggle. We were thinking we wouldn't bother his mom like we did the night before and just go back to the ER, because he could use some more fluids and he would feel better. We made it there and after the doctor saw him he said that he was having carbon dioxide getting into his body now. I told him that we knew he was terminal unless God was fixing to raise him up. He asked if we wanted to take him back home or get a hospital room and we said hospital room as we have no oxygen at home. I know now that him dying at my mom's home would not have been a good thing for mom, as she struggled with us there. As we talked about it we know that this was where he was supposed to die in the hospital with everyone around his bed. This was on Monday evening and he didn't pass away until Wednesday afternoon. He got to say goodbye one more time to his children and grandchildren.

So many people came by to see him, to pray for him to be healed, to give support to all of us. He died with dignity with cancer. I have never felt so much peace in all my life. Here the love of my life was going to heaven and I was able to help usher him in. When we first got to the room and the doctor came in. He told us that he might have five hours or less, that it would be a peaceful death – that he would just go to sleep. Rob had said that he was going to live and not die on this side of heaven. At that moment, I thought maybe we will pray him up, but I felt like I had to release him. I told Rob, I said to him, unless God is fixing to raise you up that he would be going to heaven soon. I told him that he was never going to die that he will live forever and proclaim all that the Lord has done. Immediately after I told him this he says, 'I am going to heaven' and was really excited. He was waiting for me to release him. It is true we can hold our loved ones here longer. One of the saddest days of my life was also one of the most beautiful days. I felt such love from God. I literally felt God hold me up and give me such strength. I had a peace that passes all understanding.

After all of the grandchildren and our kids and spouses came he pulled off the oxygen and said I am ready to go now. I asked him if he was afraid and he said no. It was sad but so beautiful. I can't put in words how I really felt, such peace, such calmness, almost like waiting for the presence of the Lord to come and take Him home. When he did pass the miracle was seeing his soul blow out of his body. You see he had lost his nerve on the right side of his face where the cancer was. I had wanted to see an angel take him to heaven. When he breathed his last two breaths and he was hardly breathing, but the last two breaths were forceful and he formed his mouth to the side of his face that there was no nerve. He could not do that as he had no nerve to do so. When I saw this it was like I witnessed his soul leaving his body.

I also felt a thickness leave. He even looked like he was younger. He was beautiful. **Psalm 23 KJV:**

> **The Lord is my Shepherd I shall not want. He maketh me to lie down in green pastures. He leads me beside the still waters. He restoreth my soul. He leadeth me in the paths of righteousness for his name's sake. Yea though I walk through the valley of the shadow of death I will fear no evil for thou art with me. Thy rod and thy staff they comfort me. Thou preparest a table before me in the presence of my enemies. Thou anointest my head with oil, my cup runneth over. Surely, goodness and mercy shall follow me all the days of my life and I shall dwell in the house of the Lord forever.**

I experienced God being ever present comforting me as my husband walked through the shadow of death into eternity. Free from pain, free from all the struggles that he had with the cancer over the last 2 ½ years. Healed, completely healed, and made whole. He may not have been healed on this side of heaven, but he is healed. God is always working miracles in our lives. It may not be the way we think it should be, but he gives us the grace to make it and he is with us always. He still has a plan for my life and I trust Him. He has been with me every step of the way and walks with me every day. He is my comforter, my deliverer, my soon coming king. I love him so much and I just want to serve Him and worship Him and tell others about Him and all that He has done for me. **Revelation 21.4 'And He will wipe away every tear from their eyes, and there will no longer be any death, there will no longer be any mourning, or crying or pain; the first things have passed away'.**

35

THE GLORIOUS UNFOLDING

That September after Rob's passing Amanda and I took a ten day trip to Romania to see what God was speaking to me; one of Rob's final request. At first I told him, 'you are going to heaven, I am done', but then I said I would honor his wishes. It was a beautiful time with my daughter. I was so excited to be able to show her what was in her daddy's heart. All he talked about before we actually got to go was going to Romania for several years. It was like we were in the song, 'The Glorious Unfolding'. We didn't try to figure it out, It wasn't anything like we thought the story of my life was going to be. It felt like the end had started closing in on me, but it just was not true. There is so much of the story that is still yet to unfold. I have to believe the story is so far from over. So I will hold on to every promise God has made to us and watch His glorious unfolding.

We landed in Bucharest and took a bus to Medgidia, Romania. It was a very nice visit. We stayed in an apartment with the girls that I would be coming back to stay with for four months. One of my requests to God is 'Please if I am to come don't let me stay in Romania all by myself'. After a week there we headed across the country on the train to Oradia. As we said our good-byes I knew I was coming back in January for four months. God set it all in motion right down to where I would stay, my support and plane tickets. I didn't have to do anything, but just prepare my heart and wait for the time to go.

Planting of Church in Nisipiri

One evening while in Medgidia Amanda and I were invited to go to a Bible study in a village that took place in one of the homes there. Little did we know that we would be part of a church being birthed in Nisipiri. I know Rob would have been pleased as he was always talking about planting churches, which is something he didn't get to do but was in his heart and he talked about doing some day. What a wonderful experience, His glorious unfolding of another church plant in an area of the world that had been unchurched, mostly Muslims and Orthodox. We then took an all night train to Oradia where we stayed with Simona and John for a few days and then on to Hungary and back to the states. As I sought God during this time the doors were opened for me to return to Romania for four months in 2016. I had never traveled alone, and didn't want to ever travel alone. For me to travel on a plane across the world by myself was a very big step in my life. All I wanted to do was follow the Lord and continue what was in my heart. We had sold everything to follow the Lord and now my husband was gone, but the mission work in Romania was still a very part of my heart. I knew God still had a plan for my life and I had to follow Him. My family didn't really understand. I had to go is all I know. As the time came for me to leave there was an excitement. I had no fear, absolutely no fear. I knew God was with me and that was all that mattered to me.

36

A Time to Mourn, A Time to Heal

I landed in Bucharest on January 16 and it was a cold snowy day. The girls I would be staying with and Cindy met me at the airport. I was so glad to see them. I had anticipated landing and finding my way to where they were meeting me and it was good. God guided my every step and I literally felt him right beside me. I was never afraid or scared. The first week was an adjustment. I didn't realize how much emotion would flood me as I remembered being in Medgidia with my Rob. As I would cook and get involved I would feel so overwhelmed with emotion and not wanting anyone to really know how my heart was hurting. At times I just wanted to run, but as I cried out to God he continued to give me the peace that I needed to stay and heal. I know now it was a healing time for me. As I would get involved and spend lots of time in prayer, God healed my heart.

One night after I had been in Romania for a couple of weeks I was feeling like I wanted to do more than just cook and drive. I wanted to experience people being healed and saved, an outpouring of the Holy Ghost. I had prayed to God that morning about that, 'Lord, and why am I really here?' It had already gotten dark and I had on my pajamas when a call came in from a lady in a village nearby asking for me to come and pray for her. I had not been driving much and had access to a car. I had told

Nicolette that I was a little nervous about driving out to the village and it was dark could we just pray for her over the phone. While we were waiting to decide I heard God's voice in my heart say to me, 'You shall lay hands on the sick and they shall recover' **from the scripture Mark 16.18, the later part, 'they shall lay hands on the sick, and they shall recover'.** So at this time I asked her if she had told her if we were coming or not and she said no. I said we have to go, that God had told me this and so here we go.

When we got there and she was in a lot a pain and had a fever and a headache, she had just had surgery. I had told her that whatever happens that God would be glorified, that I believed in healing and that all we have to do is believe when we pray. I prayed and then Nicolette prayed in Romanian, immediately after I prayed her ear stopped hurting and opened up, her fever left, her headache went away. She was healed, a miracle we witnessed. I then shared some of my testimony with her and found out she was not saved. I told her you can be saved tonight, that just as easy as God just healed her, He wanted to come into her heart and save her. At first she was hesitant and said, 'I will do it at church on Sunday'. I said to her, 'Why wait, Jesus is ready to come into your heart now'. So she agreed and I spoke in English, Nicolettea repeated in Romanian and then she repeated; it was three times, like the trinity. Immediately she says, 'I feel like I could fly'. I told her that God had just saved her and that is how it feels to be saved. I felt so much love towards this lady. I wanted to just stay there in the presence of the Lord.

I had been in Romania two months when one Sunday was the hardest day of my life, harder than the funeral and the time that Rob passed. The girls I was staying with were going out to the village where family was and I stayed by myself. I didn't really want to be by myself, but I knew I was to stay. They offered to stay with me, but I told them no go ahead I would be okay. My body was literally sick for several hours that day. I grieved the loss of my husband so strongly, it was at this time that I did a lot of healing. Do you know that feeling, your pain is the best way to heal? I prayed, I cried, I questioned, I almost felt like I wanted to die. The sun was shining so pretty outside and I usually like to take a walk and talk to God. I finally decided to walk to the store and get something to eat as we needed some groceries and there was really nothing to cook. As I walked down the sidewalk towards the store I was still crying and talking to God looking up at the sky. I went in and felt like I just wanted to go back to America, that I was feeling sorry for myself and mad that Rob was no longer here with me. As I came back out and was walking back the sun was getting ready to start going down. As I looked up at the sky it was so beautiful and I said to myself. I know something is up there, it was so comforting. I then took several pictures and just thanked God for the beauty and the feeling of grief just lifted and I was okay.

It was right before I left to fly back to America that I looked at the pictures and saw Jesus in the clouds. It still didn't dawn on me what I was really seeing until I got back to America and was feeling overwhelmed to adjust back to my life again and without Rob that seeing this picture comforted me. God knew when I would need this. Not only is there a picture of Jesus, but the following fall when looking at the picture again, my husband Rob is in the picture as well right above Jesus head. I can't explain it and several people say they see him too. I know Rob is with Jesus and Jesus was with me that day and is always with me. Rob is so happy and I am happy that he is with Jesus and I take comfort when I look at this picture. What an amazing feeling to know God is always with me and I am never alone. He is with all of us if we will just live for Him and trust him always, even until the ends of the earth.

37

MORNING DEVOTIONS

Each morning at the Care Center during the school week we always have devotions with the Team before we start the day. Different ones take turns each week. I had my turn more than once during this four months. As I was preparing the night before on my turn I was reading about foot-washing and wanted to share with the Team about how God uses this to heal in many different ways; physical and spiritual, and that we are told to do this in the scripture and had read the scripture about it to them. **John 13.1-17.** I had only intended to just speak about it but then I heard that still small voice that I was to offer to wash anyone's feet that wanted me to wash their feet. At first I was like really, do I have too Lord? Once I submitted I was so excited to be able to go and share this devotion and offer to wash their feet.

At first I thought I would wash Cindy's feet to demonstrate, but she did not make it to devotions that morning. Two of the women volunteered for me to wash their feet. I experienced such a love for these ladies and felt the anointing so strong. In turn, one of these women washed my feet. I needed this as much as I felt the two that volunteered needed ministering to. After it was over and the children were coming in for breakfast they then had devotions with them as well. I looked in the room where they were and the lady who was doing the devotions with the children that morning was teaching them from the scripture and was washing their feet and each other's feet. It blessed my soul to see this. That God used me that day to encourage this as in **John 13.17 KJV 'If ye know these things, happy are ye if ye do them'.** This was powerful to me that day. I was raised to do footwashing and haven't participated in several years, only something that our church does once a year at Easter. I remember we would have many times of footwashing growing up. I am not sure many people understand the humility and love and healing that comes from this if they will but submit to obeying the scripture and follow in the Lord's footsteps. Healings, forgiveness, freedom, love, and salvation comes from actively participating in doing what Jesus tells us to do.

38

SETTING UP HOUSE AGAIN

After coming back home from Romania after four months I felt like I was ready to move on to what God has called me to do. After selling my home in 2013 to be a missionary, having a place of my own again was important to me. I decided that building a home on the one lot I had left was what God was speaking to me to do. It took every bit of a year. In July 2017, I moved into my new home. It really does feel like home. I have opened my home up to missionaries and have hosted already in October a Honduran couple for a weekend and a couple from Romania. I am involved with the Romanian mission in Tortoman and my heart is there. As God leads it is my prayer for God to use me where-ever he needs me.

I am thankful to have time with my children and grandchildren. He has truly given me the desires of my heart. I hope I can be a blessing to someone today. I want to tell others about Jesus. It is important that we share the love of Jesus with our neighbor. We must be about the Father's business. I don't want to get side tracked. I pray that I will not go to the left or to the right but stay focused on His will always for my life.

God has done so much for me and He will do the same for you. You just have to put your trust in Him. He is faithful to us. Are we faithful to Him? He wants to commune with us as we spend time with him in prayer and reading our Bible. When I am down I just have me a little talk with Jesus and I find that He never left me. I just got too busy. We must communicate with Him daily. As I speak with Jesus He directs my path and starts me on my way. I want to witness the miraculous in my life. I want to see the miracles. I hope and pray that this book has encouraged you as it has me as I have read it and re-read it. I don't want to leave anything out that I need to share. It is all true and I lived it and God is so real in my life. He can be real to you. Just open up your heart and let Him in for he cares for you. He loves you so much.

39

Revelation of Passing the Mantle

Two months before Rob went to be with Jesus he shared at my daughter's church. He was saying that he had finished the race that he could not go any more, that someone else has to go; that he was passing the mantle. I assumed that the mantle would be passed to my children and grandchildren. I took Amanda with me that fall as it was her dad's wishes and then I came back and prepared to go for four months. The call to missions was still very much in my heart. I then went back to Medgidia, Romania in March of 2017 taking my grandson Timothy as his papa Rob also wanted him to go and had spoken into him about missions and following God. I just recently got back from Medgidia, Romania in March of 2018.

It was on April 15, 2018 that I read in 2 Kings 1-3 about Elijah passing the mantle to Elisha. It was an emotional moment as at this moment I realized I had picked up the mantle, that I am to continue following God's plan for my life. My heart is still in Medgidia, Romania, and as long as the Lord opens that door and my heart is wanting to go and share the Love of Jesus, then I am carrying that mantle. I know my children and grandchildren will pick it up when the time comes. A prophetic word was given on June 30, 1990 during the setting forth service before my mom and dad and brother went to Guatemala for a year. The pastor's wife at that time, Sis. Betty Fritts wrote it down and gave it to my mom.

> **Your ways I've watched. My hand weighs heavily on your life and on the lives of your children and your children's children. This night will never be from their minds – an indelible mark will it make on them. If they even try to wander away they shall not be able to. Those I have called I equip. All I want from you is your obedience and the returns shall not be able to be measured in this world – only at the hands of the King.**

Mom had put this in my Dad's Bible and while I was staying with her she remembered it and I copied it down. What a blessing to be a part of this heritage and to continue down this path of following in my parents' footsteps of doing mission work.

Just like it says if they even try to wander away they shall not be able to. As I have gotten back into my life, nothing completes me like going and working in the field, feeding the hungry, tending the sheep. I don't want to become complacent. I want to be radical for Jesus. It is not about me, it is about Jesus. What we do for Jesus is all that really matters.

40

CANCER AGAIN? 'WOW, GOD'

Just when I thought I had the ending to my book. I feel this is the 'Wow, God' experience ending. In May of 2018 I was diagnosed with breast cancer again. This is a new cancer, not recurrent. I really believed that it would have disappeared before I would have to have treatment. I prayed, I cried, I tried to understand why am I going through this again. I know for the last year I have been asking God, 'How am I to get from here to there in the plan you have for my life'. The first of January 2018 I purposed in my heart to read the Bible with Robin on Facebook. I had prayed about a Bible study to be involved in. This is literally a daily Bible study. I haven't really been preparing myself, just living my life and serving the Lord. I went to Romania in March, felt that I was doing my part as my heart is there, but I know there is something more for me to do.

As I have been going down this road again, taking chemotherapy and will be having a double mastectomy before the end of the year. It has been a learning experience. I know God could choose to heal me instantly, but he has allowed me to go through this to prepare my heart more, to pray more, to get in his word more. How can we go out and share the Gospel if we do not hide it in our heart with daily reading, not just a verse here and there. It must consume us. There has been healing come in my family with my mom through all of this, as she has sat with me and spent many nights with me and many prayers with me. I am not sure what really needed healed, just everything the last few years with sickness and losing daddy, and Rob, struggles that don't make sense but that God has healed. If it took cancer to get there then I am thankful. I just want to serve HIM and get closer. I love my family and I need my family. I had asked God to heal this and He did. He is making me into what I need to be to go out and minister to the lost and dying world. I have the answer and it is Jesus. He holds our tomorrow and we just have to trust HIM. Life happens and what we do with it when it happens is what tells the story of our faithfulness. **James 1.2-4 'Count it all joy, my brothers, when you meet trials of various kinds, for you know that the testing of your faith produces steadfastness. And let steadfastness have its full effect, that you may be perfect and complete, lacking in nothing.'**

Remember, Jesus wept in the Bible when Lazarus died. He feels our pain. He knows how hard it is and He is with us every step of the way. When I get anxious and emotional because I do, I take it to the Lord in prayer. My family has been wonderful to help me and be there for me. I feel like I want to be this strong person all the time. I know this will make me even stronger than before but while going through it I have felt so beat up and all I know is God is giving me the strength and courage to make it. With Jesus I can make it. I have to let others know that joy does come in the morning. Push through, stay the course, keep the faith. God will always show up and take care of us. It may not always go the way we think it should, but He will be there to take us through the long way if necessary. I am going the long way as I need to be closer to God and know His word and hide it in my heart that I might not sin against Him.

I am living the 'Wow, God' ending experience. To be right where I know I am to be and to feel HIS presence every step of the way. To live and not die and proclaim all that the Lord has done for me. I want the world to know that Jesus loves them and it is not His will for anyone to perish or be sick. We have to ask Him and believe and sometimes we get the miracle, sometimes it is the healing, sometimes it is the ultimate healing. Whatever we may have to face, God gives us the grace to face it. Remember He equips the called, maybe going through this is me getting more equipped to use me in a way that only comes from getting in His presence and basking in His love. **Philippians 1.6 ESV 'And I am sure of this, that he who began a good work in you will bring it to completion at the day of Jesus Christ'**. I know God is not finished with me yet, there is a longing in my heart to fulfill the work that is purposed in my heart. I can't let fear and doubt creep in. I have to stay the course focusing on HIS plan for my life.

50157019R00074

Made in the USA
Columbia, SC
02 February 2019